INDUSTRIALIZATION AND THE TRANSFORMATION OF AMERICAN LIFE

Resources for Students are available at
www.mesharpe-student.com

INDUSTRIALIZATION AND THE TRANSFORMATION OF AMERICAN LIFE

A BRIEF INTRODUCTION

JONATHAN REES

M.E.Sharpe
Armonk, New York
London, England

For Jaclyn

Library of Congress Cataloging-in-Publication Data

Rees, Jonathan, 1966–
  Industrialization and the transformation of American life : a brief introduction /
  by Jonathan Rees.
    p. cm.
  Includes bibliographical references and index.
  ISBN 978-0-7656-2255-6 (hbk. : alk. paper)—ISBN 978-0-7656-2256-3 (pbk.: alk. paper)
  1. Industrialization—Social aspects—United States—History. 2. Industrial revolution—
United States. 3. United States—Social conditions—1865–1918. 4. United States—Social
conditions—1918–1932. 5. United States—History—1865– I. Title.

HC105.R44 2012
338.0973—dc23   2012009430

Printed in the United States of America

The paper used in this publication meets the minimum requirements of
American National Standard for Information Sciences
Permanence of Paper for Printed Library Materials,
ANSI Z 39.48-1984.

IBT (c)   10   9   8   7   6   5   4   3   2   1
IBT (p)   10   9   8   7   6   5   4   3   2   1

Contents

Preface

This book comes out of my experience teaching the post-1877 American history survey course, the second part of the usual two-course introduction to this subject. I had never taken any introductory survey course myself when I first served as a teaching assistant for Stanley Schultz at the University of Wisconsin–Madison. In fact, my college and secondary school education had tended to skip just about everything from 1877, the end of Reconstruction, to some time during the 1920s. Ironically, once I became a historian, this same time period would turn out to be my favorite in all of American history. Everything was new to me at first, but even having studied it for years now I still find new things worthy of teaching that took place during this period.

The most important lesson that I learned from Professor Schultz's class was that this era is best approached topically rather than chronologically. The chronological approach is common when teaching most kinds of history because the whole subject revolves around change over time, but this is a period of weak presidents and comparatively little important legislation. Therefore, a topical approach that skips backward and forward through time illustrates the more subtle changes that have come to define modern America. Inevitably, I based my first survey course on the way Professor Schultz taught his. The longer I taught the same topics that he did—industrialization, the labor question, immigration, urbanization, and the closing of the frontier—the more I began to develop my own argument about how all these trends can be best tied together. These days I teach that industrialization and its effects are the one underlying development from this period that affected everything else that happened. This book explains that argument.

I believe that this argument is the original contribution of this book to the historiography of this period. That point aside, it is not a work of original research. This book relies heavily on the research and arguments of many other historians. In some cases, I have cited primary sources directly from their work. I have also used primary sources from this time period that I first learned about from other authors and other sources that I knew about before I even started writing. Google Books is a particularly helpful research tool for studying this period since most American works published before 1923 are available there in full (at least in the United States) since they are no longer protected by copyright. The primary sources from which I have drawn are from original materials and quotes found in the works of other historians. (In homage to one of my favorite books about part of this period, Nell Irvin Painter's *Standing at Armageddon: A Grassroots History of the Progressive Era*, I begin my citations of quotes drawn from other authors with the word "in" so as to properly recognize their contributions.) Key works on this period that I consulted but did not quote are listed in the bibliography at the back of the book.

Acknowledgments

Stanley Schultz deserves the first thanks in this work for his example of how to teach the history of this period and history in general. Thanks also go to my other professors at the University of Wisconsin–Madison who were the first ones to teach me anything about the history of this period: Rogers Hollingsworth, Diane Lindstrom, David Zonderman (who is now at North Carolina State University), and especially John Cooper. If it were not for Al Jacobs, I probably never would have heard of the naval stores industry. His book suggestions were all that I needed to write that section of the chapter on the environment. I do not know David Hounshell of Carnegie Mellon University personally, but I can mark my interest in the subject of industrialization precisely from the moment I first read his magnificent *From the American System to Mass Production, 1800–1932*. It remains the best work on this subject almost thirty years after its publication.

Finally, a word of thanks to Laurie Lieb for her terrific copyediting. She helped me better explain many of my points and this book is vastly improved for her having worked on it.

Introduction

In 1869 two psychologists working independently coined the term "neurasthenia," a new ailment that they attributed to the fast pace of modern life. In 1881, one of those psychologists, George Beard, wrote a book called *American Nervousness*. Beard's work, a mostly scientific treatise, actually popularized the condition. Beard suggested that Americans were more likely to get "certain physical forms of hysteria," including "hay fever, sick headache[s] . . . and some forms of insanity" because of this ailment. In Beard's estimation, "No age, no country, and no form of civilization, not Greece, nor Rome, nor Spain, nor the Netherlands, in the days of their glory, possessed such maladies."[1] Modern industry played a particularly important role in causing neurasthenia, Beard explained. "Manufacturers, under the impulses of steam power and invention," he wrote, "have multiplied the burdens of mankind; and railways, telegraphs, canals, steamships, and the utilization of steam power in agriculture, and in handling and preparing materials for transportation, have made it possible to transact a hundred-fold more business in a limited time than even in the eighteenth century."[2] To many this was progress, but Beard described the costs that this kind of progress inflicted on many Americans.

While Beard was not the only late nineteenth-century observer to lament the substantial changes that permeated daily life in this era, what separated his conception of American nervousness from other critiques was his emphasis on the physical manifestations of modernization. So much was changing so fast in the United States that other critics simply did not know where to start when trying to understand the toll that economic progress inflicted upon society. Beard and other psychologists, on the other hand, did not try to define the exact nature of these changes on the wider world. They looked only at how these changes affected individuals rather than society as a whole. To these scientists and many others, the human body itself was a machine, and their job was to fix it. They thought that the human machine ran on "nervous energy." Neurasthenia was a sign that that energy had been entirely expended while trying to cope with the other machines that came to define the age.

A BOON FOR ALL BRAIN WORKERS.

For Nervous Headaches, for Impaired Eyesight, for Railway
Passengers, Editors, Lawyers, Professors, Authors,
Merchants, Book-keepers, Business Men, Business
Ladies, Architects, Active Salesmen, and all
Brain Workers, in Every Capacity of
Life, will find, upon trial, that

Hill's Genuine Magnetic Anti-Headache Cap

Is a Brain-food Unequalled in the Known World. It

furnishes and supplies Nature's demands, viz., Magnetism, which moves
the blood in our veins, the muscles and the nerves of our bodies.

These caps are made of silk and contain twenty-two (22) of **Hill's Grand
Medal Magnetic Storage Batteries,** polarized and scientifically arranged, so that each will furnish positive and negative currents of pure Magnetism to the brain, flesh and blood. They never produce shocks or sores like
'Electric' devices, but always soothe, strengthen and invigorate. They furnish
Nature's remedy for insomnia. The superior curative powers of Hill's Magnetic
Appliances are well known throughout the land, with bushels of testimonials for
such as desire. The price of this cap is only $3.00. Will be mailed to any
address in the U. S., with postage prepaid, on receipt of the price, in M. O. or
registered letter. Give size of hat worn, and address

HILL MAGNETIC APPLIANCE CO.,

READING, MASS.

The anti-headache cap was just one of many devices that charlatans created to treat
neurasthenia, a medical condition that illustrated the effects of industrialization on the
people who experienced it. *(Courtesy of Library of Congress)*

Like Beard, a few historians have tried to examine the effects of industrialization during the nineteenth century. Yet despite its extraordinary impact, industrialization remains a very abstract concept to most scholars because it is harder to imagine that process than to describe its many effects. This might explain why industrialization does not get much space in many American history textbooks. Since the late nineteenth century was not rife with strong political or military leaders, historians have fewer traditional subjects from this time period to write about. The sharp increase in immigration, the growth of large cities, and an acceleration of the movement to the American West are trends that are harder to explain than laws or wars. Industrialization underlies all the general developments of this era, yet it is hard to appreciate precisely how that process affected these developments because the impacts of industrialization were so broad. With hindsight, we can examine one trend at a time. By doing this, connections between the better-examined aspects of this era and the phenomenon of industrialization become clear.

The goal of what follows is to show how industrialization was at the center of the major historical developments of the late nineteenth and early twentieth centuries. This book describes precisely how industrialization occurred on the shop floor of American workplaces and the many impacts that it had at those workplaces and on the society at large. This is not a volume about why industrialization occurred, which is an interesting question well worth answering, but which would require a closer examination of an earlier period, before the impact of industrialization became completely clear. Answering that question would also require an international perspective, while this book concentrates upon the impact of this phenomenon on just American history. While such restrictions might seem unduly limiting for the study of such a monumental global phenomenon, these conditions are crucial in order to examine such a complex process. Too much context, and there will be no space for detail in what follows. Too much detail, and there will be no space for context.

What Is Industrialization?

The late nineteenth and early twentieth centuries were the era of industrialization in the United States. While this process began earlier in the nineteenth century, industrialization accelerated greatly in the decades following the Civil War. Historians generally acknowledge that industrialization was an enormously important process, but there is really no agreement on exactly what this process was. Most historians do not even bother to define the term "industrialization," let alone explain the concept to their readers. Those who do tackle the word often fail to understand what they are trying to define. That is why any discussion of industrialization needs to begin with a clear and precise definition of this term.

Industrialization was (and still is) a process—two processes, actually: mechanization and the division of labor. Both of these processes reflect different kinds of industrializing, and in the period covered in this work both kinds of industrialization happened. While we will see that these are two distinct processes, they both have the same effect—an increase in production. Industrialization produces more stuff. Each of these phenomena—the division of labor, the mechanization, and the additional stuff produced by these processes—had transformative effects upon American society. In order to understand those effects, though, it is necessary to define the two processes more precisely and to describe the extraordinary degree to which industrialization in its heyday increased production.

Let us begin with the division of labor. In preindustrial societies, one worker generally performed all the tasks necessary to make a particular good. However, once the labor became divided, each person would do the same small task over and over again instead of many different tasks. This division of labor not only saved on the time needed to change from one task to another (thereby increasing production), but also made it easier to train workers since an employee need only perform one task rather than many. This simplification of on-the-job activities often made it possible for an employer to lower wages since every less-skilled worker could be easily replaced by someone who needed little training. Skilled workers got higher wages because there were generally fewer people available with whom they could be replaced. Industries that required skilled workers were often the last ones to industrialize.

How did the division of labor change what workers did every day? It meant that instead of doing many things, they would do one thing repeatedly. The quintessential example of the division of labor comes from England approximately 100 years before the opening of the era covered in this book. In his 1776 classic *The Wealth of Nations*, Adam Smith describes how the division of labor affected the operation of an English pin factory. "One man draws out the wire," he wrote; "another straights it, a third cuts it, a fourth points it, a fifth grinds it at the top for receiving the head . . . the important business of making a pin is, in this manner, divided into about eighteen distinct operations." The significance of this change in operations came from the increase in productivity it provided: "Those ten persons . . . could make among them upwards of forty-eight thousand pins in a day. But if they had all wrought separately and independently, and without any of them having been educated to this particular business, they certainly could not each of them have made twenty, perhaps not one pin a day."[3] No machines of any kind were needed to vastly improve the productive capacity of pin making. Simply using labor differently could make the operation much more efficient. This is why the division of labor tended to predate mechanization over the history of industrialization, as dividing labor did not require any technological breakthroughs.

While the owners of factories benefited by selling the fruits of increased production and their customers benefited from the drop in price that a surplus of goods made possible, few workers got to keep the benefits of the surplus they created. Indeed, by the time George Beard wrote *American Nervousness*, the disadvantages of the division of labor for workers were abundantly clear. "The effect of this exclusive concentration of mind and muscle to one mode of action through months and years," Beard wrote, "is . . . pernicious, and notably so, when reenforced, as it almost universally is, by the bad air of overheated and ill-ventilated establishments. Herein is one unanticipated cause of the increase of insanity and other diseases of the nervous system among the laboring and poorer classes."[4] While many workers obviously performed specialized tasks without going insane, it should also be obvious that doing the same thing over and over again throughout the working day is not nearly as engaging or rewarding as doing many different things. The division of labor also eliminated the sense of pride that skilled craft workers developed when seeing production through from beginning to end. When people became totally divorced from the product of their labor, morale often plummeted. That likely hindered their effort, but the effects of mechanization easily made up for the negative effects of the division of labor on motivation.

Mechanization, as the word suggests, simply means the replacement of workers with machines. While today we often hear about robot arms or computers doing the work that humans used to do, mechanization was something new during the era of industrialization. In fact, the division of labor often aided the process of industrialization because dividing a job into discrete tasks was often the first step in creating a machine that could do the same task better and/or faster than a human being. Since there were plenty of inefficiently human-performed tasks in countless industries that manufacturers wanted to mechanize, this kind of industrialization was largely new at this time. The cost-savings brought by industrialization could be staggering. The E.P. Allis Company of Milwaukee, which manufactured steam engines and industrial equipment, first began to employ electric cranes inside its factory in 1890. It was the first firm in America to use these large, expensive machines. They quickly proved their worth since they allowed the company to cut sixty workers whose main job had been to move parts from one part of the building to another.

Yet mechanization had greater ramifications than simply putting people out of work. Writing in 1904, the economist Thorstein Veblen referred to the "the discipline of the machine process," suggesting that mechanization permeated many aspects of American society far away from the factory. "The machine process pervades the modern life and dominates it in a mechanical sense," he argued. "Its dominance is seen in the enforcement of precise measurements and adjustment and the reduction of all manner of things, purposes and acts, necessities, conveniences and amenities of life, to standard units."⁵ Obviously, this process fell hardest on the workers who tended the machines, responding to bells and whistles at the beginning of the working day when these devices needed them. The railroad timetable was perhaps the most obvious example of this phenomenon outside the factory gate, but Veblen also saw that machines created habits of mind in all who came in contact with them. They promoted values like efficiency and productivity rather than relaxation or contemplation.

Both these aspects of industrialization—the division of labor and mechanization—had the same result: a sharp increase in manufactured goods. When this increase was great enough, the result was called something that sounds much more impressive: mass production. Starting in the 1880s, most modern factories were set up to produce goods as a continuous process. Their machinery was so sophisticated that it practically cranked out product all by itself. Cigarettes, breakfast cereals, photographic film—items that had once required considerable labor expenses could now be made so cheaply that people who might not have thought otherwise about buying them could fit them into the family budget. Mass distribution through railroads, steamships, and other forms of industrialized transportation brought the product of these new factories to people all across America and around the world.

There could have been no mass production without mass consumption (or vice versa, for that matter). With more stock on hand, produced at a low price, manufacturers drastically cut prices and could still make a considerable profit on their wares because they sold to more people than ever before. Henry Ford, a genius not just in the production of cars, but in explaining the principles behind production in general, understood this particularly well. "I will build a car for the great multitude," he wrote upon the introduction of his Model T in 1908. "It will be large enough for the family but small enough for the individual to run and care for . . . [I]t will be so low in price that no man making a good salary will be unable to own one—and enjoy with his family the blessing of hours in God's great open spaces." Ford also understood that the benefits of industrialization went well beyond the ability to travel. "Gradually," he noted near the end of the era of industrialization, "under the benign influence of American industry, wives are released from work, little children are no longer exploited; and given more time, they both become free to go out and find new products, new merchants, and manufacturers who are supplying them. . . . Machinery is accomplishing in the world what man has failed to do by preaching, propaganda or the written word."[6] Ford's assembly line made this possible by enabling his dealers to sell cheaper automobiles. By 1913 a Ford Model T cost just $500—hundreds less than the competition.[7]

The Model T symbolizes the primary benefit of industrialization. Mass-produced goods improved the quality of life of everyone who could afford them, but not the hand-crafted versions of similar products. Automobiles were rich people's toys before Ford developed the Model T. Once the great multitude could afford them, their lives became better. This explains why so many people readily accepted the difficult circumstances created by industrialization that are described in this book. To them the advantages of industrialization outweighed the negative effects. By providing investment opportunities and by lowering the cost of living, industrialization created the modern American middle class. A rising tide really did lift all boats. However, it lifted some boats much higher than others.

The Early History of Industrialization

The benefits of mass consumption explain why a process as disruptive as industrialization was to the normal rhythms of life was not feared, but welcomed. Many people thought industrialization was liberating because not all the effects were clear at the onset of the process. People often refer to the process of industrialization as "The Industrial Revolution." This term is misleading. While the word "revolution" accurately conveys the significance of the changes that this process brought, it also suggests a suddenness that simply does not apply here. Political revolutions, for example, often seem out-of-the-blue to the citizens who are affected by them. Industrialization was a very slow process, but one with tremendously important implications. Many historians associate industrialization with the birth of modern capitalism itself since the creation of surplus products required a global search for both raw materials and markets. Its effects were far-reaching even before it began in the United States or directly affected the majority of Americans.

The roots of industrialization go back long before the period studied here. This process began in Great Britain during the eighteenth century. It depended upon two parallel developments: mechanical innovations in the country's textile industry and great improvements in the technology that generated the power to run them, namely steam engines. In 1789 an operative named Samuel Slater emigrated from England to Rhode Island. He had used his six years of apprenticeship in an English textile factory to learn the British system, and now he re-created that system in the unique circumstances of New England. In the years following the War of 1812, Francis Cabot Lowell created a new system, more closely patterned on the British system since Lowell did his best to copy machines he had seen on a prewar trip to England and because he put spinning and weaving under one roof, as the British did. Lowell, Massachusetts, the city his associates named after him shortly following his untimely death in 1820, quickly became the most important textile-manufacturing locale in the world. Other important American industries that grew as a result of mechanization and the division of labor in the early nineteenth century included clock making, gun manufacturing, and shoe making. The other great British innovation that made industrialization possible was the development of the steam engine. The first was a gigantic machine developed by Thomas Newcomen to pump water out of flooded mines. James Watt improved on this model, making it smaller and more efficient. American inventors would make more improvements to it still.

Industrialization began in America about 1815. While some industries like textiles and clock making were heavily industrialized during the first half of the nineteenth century, industrialization did not really spread throughout American manufacturing until after the Civil War. There were several reasons for this delay. One was the time it took to perfect the machinery involved in creating any product. It also took many years to achieve enough improvements in transportation to make the raw materials of the American West accessible to the manufacturers of the East. Added incentive came from the need to supply the vast Union Army during the Civil War. The destruction brought on by that conflict wasted American resources, but also the war spurred the process of industrialization in the sense that it encouraged new production techniques that would have their greatest impact once the war ended. Only after the war did inventors like Thomas Edison develop the notion of systematic invention, the idea that science should be used to make money rather than to increase the store of human knowledge. This meant that scientists like Edison invariably became entrepreneurs, examining not just what they could invent, but how to make money doing it. Lastly, only after the Civil War were the nation's railroads extensive enough to guarantee a means to distribute all the excess product created by industrialized factories across many industries.

The late nineteenth- and early twentieth-century acceleration of industrialization is the reason that this book focuses on the period between 1865 and 1920. This was the heyday of that process. More industries began to industrialize as technology improved. The result of more industrialization was yet more production and greater economic activity aimed at distributing and selling that product. As industrialization increased, the effects of industrialization strengthened and spread throughout the economy too. The early history of industrialization changed America to some degree, but it is primarily important as a precedent for what would come later. Rather than affecting just a few industries, later industrialization completely transformed American life. This single multifaceted, far-reaching development came to define modern life. To try to understand the late nineteenth and early twentieth centuries without understanding the importance of industrialization is like trying to watch a play in which all the main character's lines are read from offstage. You cannot understand the story without seeing the center of the action.

An Episodic Approach to Industrialization

The effects of industrialization are visible in nearly every aspect of the history of this period. That means there are many possible entry points for discussing this subject. So many history textbooks present their subject as a series of unrelated facts. Politicians and politics get their own subheading. Railroads and the opening of the West get another. If the textbook was written relatively recently, the influence of new historical subfields such as environmental history or women's history might be there too. What is often lacking, though, is any kind of glue that ties these facts together. Industrialization is the link that unites nearly all of the history of this period. There are important aspects of American history that are not covered in this book to the extent they deserve. The histories of race and gender during this time period are two important examples. Industrialization cannot explain everything, but it is an important influence upon so much going on in America during this time that it deserves the central position that this book gives it. Even the effects of industrialization upon race and gender could be considered, but trends that have a more obvious relationship to this process are the main topics of what follows.

A history of every aspect and effect of industrialization would be too big to fit into one small book. For one thing, it would require describing an awful lot of industries. This would obscure the interesting similarities across industries. For this subject then, less can be more. Rather than try to tell the story of industrialization in every American industry, examples from a few of those industries—some big, some small—will follow. This allows us to get at the underlying concepts and the often-repeated effects that make industrialization so historically significant. Mechanization, for example, was important during this earlier era because no worker wanted to be replaced by a machine, but employers preferred machines to people if the machine could do similar or better work at the same cost. That dynamic and its effect on employment remain important today for precisely the same reason.

In order to get at these underlying concepts in a limited number of pages, this book approaches the history of industrialization in America episodically. Instead of being organized chronologically, as are most history books, it is organized topically. That means that what follows covers the history of the same years by looking at them from different perspectives. This episodic approach is absolutely crucial for capturing underlying changes and the effect of those changes on numerous and varied aspects of American life. It is not necessary to describe every resource that industrial enterprises extracted to demonstrate that resource extraction was a historically significant activity. It is not necessary to explain how machines replaced people in every industry to conclude that this phenomenon was historically significant too. In these sample arguments, a few examples can suffice.

Each chapter is organized around a question designed to suggest the importance of industrialization to the broader history of this period—social, political, environmental, and so on. In most cases it is necessary to examine both the process of industrialization itself and its effects together in order to demonstrate the central importance of industrialization to the history of this era. After discussing the answer to the question, three seemingly different but in fact related historical examples are considered in order to explain that answer. One historical example might be a fluke. A second similar anecdote might be a coincidence. However, three similar stories suggest a trend caused or greatly impacted by a common source—namely, industrialization. It is only through understanding such relationships that the extraordinary historical importance of industrialization fully emerges. To find more historical examples of this trend will require more research. Examples from other sources will not be hard to find as long as you understand the importance of the broader concepts illustrated in what follows.

Notes

1. George M. Beard, *American Nervousness: Its Causes and Consequences* (New York: G.P. Putnam's Sons, 1881), vii–viii.

2. Beard, 115–116.

3. Adam Smith, *An Inquiry Into the Nature and Causes of the Wealth of Nations* (Chicago: University of Chicago Press, 1976), 8–9.

4. Beard, 102.

5. Thorstein Veblen, *The Theory of Business Enterprise* (New York: Charles Scribner's Sons, 1919), 306, reprint.

6. In Stephen Watts, *The People's Tycoon: Henry Ford and the American Century* (New York: Random House, 2005), 19, 136.

7. Watts, 146.

INDUSTRIALIZATION AND THE TRANSFORMATION OF AMERICAN LIFE

Varieties of Industrialization

Q. *Why and how did industrialization
affect industries differently?*

Industrialization happened most often in factories. "A factory," explained the economist Carroll Wright in 1882, "is an establishment where several workmen are collected together . . . for producing results by their combined efforts, which they could not accomplish separately; and for saving the loss of time which the carrying of an article from place to place, during the several processes necessary to complete its manufacture, would occasion."[1] Even this shortened version of Wright's definition covers a lot of territory. Many concepts and ideas that shaped industrialization crossed industries during this era. Nevertheless, the exact manner in which industrialization changed the process of manufacturing differed from factory to factory. Sometimes it was different at different facilities that produced the same things. Sometimes it was different in different countries. Industrialization in America proceeded at different rates in different regions (although most of it was concentrated in the Northeast). What is important is that the same external forces that created industrialization affected every industry and nearly every factory differently, wherever it happened to be located.

It is difficult to master the exact details of the production process in one industry, let alone all industries in an economy. Given such limitations, making cross-industrial comparisons allows us to understand common principles that affected industrialization in the late nineteenth and early twentieth centuries and that continue to affect the American economy down to this day. Similar technologies developed across industries over time. Sometimes people applied old technologies to new uses. For example, both arms manufacturers and sewing machine producers entered the bicycle making business during the 1880s as a second (or sometimes third) line of production because the technology needed to make the components was so similar. Likewise, Thomas Edison got many of his ideas for other inventions simply by working on improving telegraphy. Henry Ford claimed that the inspiration for his assembly line came from the "disassembly" lines in the meatpacking industry. In short, the inspiration needed to produce anything more efficiently can come from a wide range of circumstances.

This chapter (and to a certain extent the rest of this book) will examine such similarities as well as differences between industrial processes. Despite the many differences involved, a few concepts can help the reader assess the nature of industrialization at production sites in different industries, even at different times. Understanding how this works requires a review of these concepts as we begin to examine these processes in a few sample industries.

The definition of industrialization as offered in the introduction to this book is illustrated in Figure 1.1. In this depiction, the size of the arrows between "Mechanization" and "More Stuff" and between "Division of Labor" and "More Stuff" is equal, thereby implying that the impact of these elements on overall production was equal. However, this was not necessarily the case.

Early on in the history of industrialization, textile manufacturers farmed out their work to many operatives who worked at home. About 1815 many American textile manufacturers increased the productive capacity of their operations simply by bringing together operations under one roof. This made it easier to divide labor and benefit from lower transportation costs. Mechanization was available at larger operations, but these smaller operations benefited primarily from the division of labor. Later in the century, production tended to increase more from mechanization than from division of labor. Different mixes of the division of labor and mechanization changed the way any particular business operated, therefore changing the effects it had on society as a whole.

The largest economic actors stood to benefit the most from the division of labor because they had the most labor to divide. Large factories also stood to benefit most from mechanization because they were most likely to have the money to buy expensive machines. Therefore, the size of an operation had an enormous impact on the degree to which its industrialization could affect society at large. In many cases, factories had to be extraordinarily large to gain the optimal benefit from industrializing. The name for this tendency is "economies of scale."

While it is impossible to cover every factory in every industry, three factories in three important industries can serve as prototypes. The first

Figure 1.1

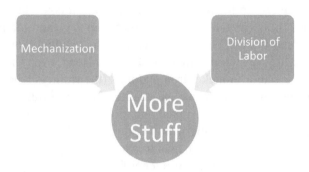

example is a plant in an industry that depended primarily upon mechanization during the later stages of industrialization. The second example comes from an industry that depended primarily on the division of labor. The third example comes from an industry that exhibited a good balance between both principles. In the course of examining these factories, it will be possible to illustrate how some of the principles related to industrialization applied to these industries and to begin to discuss the effects of these operations.

The Edgar Thomson Works of the Carnegie Steel Company

Steel mills are perhaps the quintessential example of late nineteenth-century industrialization because of their importance to the American economy and because of their dependence upon mechanization. Indeed, the contribution of mechanization to the industrialization of steelmaking was much greater than the contribution of the division of labor because mechanization allowed steelmaking to operate on a much larger scale than ever before. That difference greatly affected the operation of the industry and therefore changed the nature of its impact on American society. To understand this impact, it is necessary to recognize that steelmakers sold their product not to consumers, but to producers of other goods. Mass marketing of steel was impossible, but mass production was possible thanks to a series of technological innovations that reflected the principles of industrialization across industries. The firm that came to be named the Carnegie Steel Company pioneered many of these innovations.

Steel, of course, is a substance that has been made for many centuries. However, up to the mid-nineteenth century it could be made only in small batches. The reason for this limitation was the time needed to produce it and the difficulty that even the most skilled workers faced when working. Most companies made iron instead, even though it required skilled labor to make. Iron puddlers (the workers who made the judgments needed to guarantee the quality of a successful batch of iron or steel) were among the best paid and most respected members of the mid-nineteenth-century American working class. The invention of the Bessemer converter in 1856 began to change that. These devices made it possible to make steel in large batches for the first time by blowing air through the molten slag that came out of a blast furnace. This process guaranteed a successful batch (a superior batch to hand-puddled steel, in fact) every time. It also greatly increased the amount of steel that one facility could produce. With an increased supply of steel and lower labor costs (since steelmaking facilities no longer required puddlers), steel prices dropped sharply. Because iron and steel were close substitutes, steel quickly came to replace the much softer and more brittle iron in important products like railroad ties and tall buildings.

Industrialization also included the reorganization of the entire production process. At the same time the Bessemer converter and its replacement, the open hearth furnace, came into use, the entire layout of steel factories changed thanks to the willingness of the industrialist Andrew Carnegie to experiment with new technology. Carnegie never worked in a steel mill, but his desire to increase production beyond any of his competitors quickly made his firm the largest in the industry. Better technology led him to build the largest Bessemer steel plant in America, the Edgar Thomson Works, in 1875. Over time, however, his engineers improved on the process by shortening the steps needed to get steel from the blast furnace into the converters. Not content with merely improving efficiency, Carnegie's company also pioneered the use of open-hearth technology. This process not only improved the quality of the steel that emerged from it, but further decreased the need for skilled labor to operate it. Carnegie used his technological advantage to lower his prices and thereby undercut his competitors. He bought up those competitors whom he did not drive out of business.

The jobs of skilled labor were not divided away at Edgar Thomson. Instead they were automated away. While a puddling mill had as many as fifty skilled workers making iron, a single blower could operate the machinery that covered the same function in a Bessemer steel mill. Puddlers could determine whether iron had reached the proper consistency only by sight and feel, but in an open-hearth furnace frequent samples were taken and analyzed in a laboratory in order to achieve the same result. What made mechanization more important to the industrialization process in steel mills than in most other industries, however, was that many jobs for unskilled workers actually met this same fate too. Human labor was a bottleneck in the continuous operation of steel production. The introduction of skip hoists (small cars or buckets that carried the coke, iron, and other materials needed to make steel from the bottom to the top of a furnace for melting), for example, eliminated a considerable amount of unskilled labor at both ends of the line and thereby improved the efficiency of the entire steelmaking process.

In essence, the division of labor for the workers who tended these machines was an afterthought. Even then, the job of the steelworkers in a Bessemer or open-hearth mill was more complicated than just tending machines. Each part of a steel mill was in continuous operation in order to maximize production. Therefore, workers at each stage of the process had to coordinate with those in front and behind them in order to make sure that production ran smoothly. Although less skilled than puddlers, these workers still had to have diagnostic skill to ensure the continuity of the production process; they could not zone out like those doing repetitive work on an assembly line. They had to keep their mind on how other parts of the production process affected what they did in order for the mill to maintain peak efficiency. The result was not the creation of a new pool of unskilled workers, but a blending of jobs to create a population of machine operators that could rightfully be described as "semiskilled."

Carnegie, unlike other businessmen of his time, wrote about the changes going on in his industry and others in abstract terms. By doing so, he not only demonstrated his intellect, but justified his policies. In his most famous essay, "The Gospel of Wealth," written in 1889, he explained how changes "in the manufacture of products" had changed the world for the better by allowing the poor to "enjoy what the rich could not before afford. What were the luxuries have become the necessaries of life. The laborer has now more comforts than the farmer had a few generations ago."[2] For a time this was the case for Carnegie's employees, but when his company faced greater competition during the late 1880s, their situation became dire.

Once Andrew Carnegie bought the Homestead Steel Works outside of Pittsburgh, he made it the most technologically sophisticated steel works in the world. *(Courtesy of the Library of Congress)*

Unlike other steel manufacturers, Carnegie recognized the Amalgamated Association of Iron and Steel Workers union in some of his mills. In 1886 he wrote, "My experience has been that trade-unions upon the whole are beneficial to both labor and to capital."[3] However, when the market for the steel rails in which his firm specialized turned sour, Carnegie Steel had to upgrade its facilities in order to switch from steel rails to structural steel for buildings and armor plate, the products that steel customers demanded most starting in the late 1880s. These technological improvements made recognizing the union unnecessary. The Amalgamated Association generally did not object to technological improvements at the mills it represented, but one exception to this rule proved to be Carnegie's Homestead Steel Works in 1892. In order to break the union, Carnegie's partner Henry Clay Frick refused to negotiate a new contract with the union workers and locked them and every nonunion worker out of the mill on July 1, 1892. On July 6, the strikers started a gun battle with a barge of Pinkerton guards hired to protect replacements for striking workers. The result was twelve deaths (three Pinkertons, nine strikers) and the summoning of the Pennsylvania National Guard to restore order. That kind of death toll is almost unequaled for a single incident in American labor history. However, even a clash of great significance like this one did not stem the tide toward the virtual eradication of trade unions in the steel industry. They did not return until 1937. Carnegie Steel industrialized in order to take advantage of the remarkable gains in production that these processes brought. The destruction of trade unions was just a financially advantageous side effect.

The Triangle Shirtwaist Company

Textile manufacturing was one of the first American industries to industrialize. The sewing machine debuted during the 1850s, but could do only a limited amount of work in the early twentieth-century garment trade. This industry depended upon the division of labor to drive production. The Triangle Shirtwaist Company of New York City was the largest and most established garment-making operation in the city during this era. It would become infamous because of what happened to the mostly female workers there during one tragic day in 1911.

The garment industry consisted of the businesses that took those textiles and turned them into wearable clothes. Unlike industries that depended upon the efficiencies of mass production to drive costs down, garment firms produced their product in batches. Firms that operated in this manner could not depend upon economies of scale or a first mover advantage to gain economic advantage. As a result, they were generally small. They could not depend upon mass distribution to market whatever they produced either.

Retailers would call for a specific number of garments to be delivered by a particular date. The number and the kind of garment in the order often depended upon the particular season. Unlike those produced by tailors, these kinds of garments were not custom-made. Nevertheless, the producers tried to keep up with styles even as they kept costs low. A successful garment-making firm might not be successful very long if the nature of the market changed over time. In order to accommodate rapid changes in products, clothing manufacture was generally farmed out to small shops in small batches.

Many of these small shops were based in New York City, the center of the American garment industry. Competition was fierce, and the easiest way to save money was to scrimp on labor costs because labor made up most of the cost of a garment. For example, the shop where Rose Cohen got her first job had four sewing machines and had sixteen people in it. Other workers had their own sewing machine that they carried from job to job. Many sewing machines were powered by foot pedals rather than electricity. Therefore, almost every kind of sewing was still exhausting, labor-intensive work.

The garment industry needed hundreds and thousands of workers. For small operations, those workers were often married women who would sew at home while simultaneously looking after their children and/or boarders. They were paid a piece rate for each garment they finished, and often the children helped too. Other women worked through what was known as the task system, as part of a group of friends and neighbors. These teams depended upon the division of labor. William Leiserson, an industrial relations investigator, described how they operated. "There would be a team or 'set' composed of a Baster, Half Baster, Operator, Helper, Finisher, Trimmer, Bushelman, and Presser," he explained. "All these were paid by the week but the team had to turn out a certain amount of work every day. The contractor took advantage of the absence of the union and constantly added to the day's task."[4] The contractors who benefited most from this homework were not employers but middlemen between the laborers and the manufacturers who sold the products to retailers. Rather than invest in factories of their own, the middlemen got workers to turn their homes into factories.

As demand increased over time, clothing companies gradually moved from homework to having their employees work in factories where the pace of production could be better controlled. Such workplaces bore little resemblance to the facilities owned by Henry Ford or Andrew Carnegie. The smaller ones were often dark, poorly ventilated rooms in overcrowded neighborhoods. Larger ones might be nothing but a few rooms in a tenement house. People slept during the night and sewed in the same place they slept. Their apartments were their factories. Like the factories that made cars or furniture, these shops utilized the division of labor too. Unlike those larger factories, the garment shops absolutely depended upon it.

The most important advantage of the garment industry's sweatshop system was flexibility. Since demand for garments changed with the season, many workers were employed on a temporary basis. With little capital, the employers needed only to hire the necessary number of workers to complete a particular contract. There were few economies of scale and no mechanical fix that would vastly increase productive efficiency. The easiest way to increase production was to hire more workers. After all, they could be fired without warning after demand for their services decreased. Businesses with heavy machinery had to continue operating because of their fixed costs. Garment contractors could disappear and return at a different location overnight.

A shirtwaist was a woman's blouse tailored like a man's shirt. Unlike other fashionable garments, the need for this item was not just seasonal, so there was steady work all year. Therefore, shirtwaists tended to be mass-produced in factories rather than assembled through piecework in workers' own apartments. Like most large New York City garment firms, the Triangle Shirtwaist Company tended to hire young immigrant girls to do most of the sewing it needed. The number of workers there doubled during the first decade of the twentieth century. It was spread over the top three floors of a ten-story high-rise office building in the Manhattan garment district.

This layered arrangement was not a typical factory, but it provided enough space for the multiple operations needed to make clothing. On each floor, the workers sat at rows of tables with sewing machines on them. Each worker did the same task on each garment and then passed it along to the next station. Children might start in the garment industry by simply cutting threads off finished garments. Later they might get promoted to other departments in the same building. The cutting department, for eample, cut the embroidery to be inserted into the shirtwaist. Since every department at the Triangle Shirtwaist Company was crammed into just three floors of a single building, the partial garments could be quickly transported to the next step in the production process.

The owners of such factories cared little for their employees. What mattered was continuing to produce a steady stream of garments to meet the needs of the manufacturers they supplied. Since most of the workers in this industry were paid by each piece they finished, they were supposed to be self-motivated. As one of them wrote in reference to another firm in 1902, "The machines go like mad all day because the faster you work the more money you get. Sometimes in my haste I get my finger caught and the needle goes right through it. It goes so quick, though, that it does not hurt much. I bind the finger up with a piece of cotton and go on working. We all have accidents like that."[5] Workers often complained that they were treated like just another machine. Indeed, with the problem of motivation solved by the piecework system, in some sense they were. This explains why companies like Triangle did so little for their employees' safety.

The notorious Triangle Shirtwaist fire, in which 146 of the company's approximately 500 employees died, was the natural extension of the

The Triangle Shirtwaist fire, which led to the death of 146 workers, was the deadliest industrial accident in the history of New York City and provided the impetus for new industrial safety laws at the state and federal levels.

dehumanizing impulse behind industrialization. On March 25, 1911, the fire broke out in a pile of rags on the factory floor near the machinery. Unlike the meatpacking process, which used "everything but the squeal" from the pig, garment factories produced lots of scrap fabric and lint, since only the human eye could judge the irregular patterns needed to cut and stitch the garments together. To clear the piles of debris regularly would have taken the workers away from their labor far too often for management's taste. Instead, the piles accumulated and periodically caught fire. There had been seven fires at the Triangle Company during the previous decade alone. Still, the owners did not protect their lightly capitalized factory space from fire. When this tragedy struck, firefighters arrived quickly on the scene, but their ladders were not tall enough to reach stranded workers. Many of the workers jumped to their death out of nine- and ten-story windows because the exit doors had been locked to prevent them from taking unscheduled bathroom breaks that interrupted production. The vast majority of the victims were young immigrant girls. Some were as young as fifteen years old.

Demonstrating its flexibility, Triangle reestablished itself at a new location three days after the fire, just as if nothing had ever happened. Shortly after that, the owners of the shop were indicted for first- and second-degree manslaughter for keeping those exit doors locked. They were acquitted. The story of the fire and especially pictures of the bodies of the victims spurred reform. Ironically, fire safety had been one aim of a major strike throughout the garment industry just two years before. Had the union organized the factory, this tragedy might not have happened. At least the tragedy inspired a series of state-level labor reforms that made all factories in New York safer.

The Washburn "A" Flour Mill

Unlike many other industries of that time, flour milling in the late nineteenth century depended upon both mechanization and the division of labor at the same time to produce its product. Machines could do what workers could not do, but many workers were still needed to operate them. The origins of automatic flour mills dated back to the earliest years of industrialization. In 1782 Oliver Evans of Delaware invented five machines that partially automated the production of flour from wheat. As important as the concept of automation would prove to be for industrialization across industries later on, Evans's mill was on such a small scale (and was only operated seasonally) that it did little to change the American grain milling industry. The real change came in the late 1870s when millers around Minneapolis, Minnesota, developed a new system that largely automated flour production on a much larger scale. Cadwallader C. Washburn built his first mill along the Mississippi River at St. Anthony's Fall in 1866. This was his "B," a name that suggests the experimental nature of the place (otherwise it would have been named "A"). Washburn completed his second and final, heavily industrialized "A" mill in 1879.

The initial problem that any miller faced was how to break the hard outside part of the wheat, called the germ, so as to get at the soft endosperm inside. White flour, then the most expensive and most coveted flour, is made entirely from endosperm. Washburn, along with his Minneapolis competitor Charles A. Pillsbury, solved this problem and produced white flour on a mass scale. By doing so, they changed the way Americans ate. These Minneapolis millers did this by introducing what came to be known as the gradual reduction process, a technique they borrowed from Hungary. Their companies replaced large millstones to grind wheat with a series of porcelain or iron rollers. The grain would be ground to increasingly finer portions depending upon how many of these rollers it went through. The portions of the grain that had been a waste product before, the outside portion or "middlings," could now be collected by means of a purifier that would separate them with a puff of air and then move them to where they could be ground again into a usable product. Because of this process, it became much easier and cheaper for flour companies to make white flour.

The way milling firms arranged their machines in the mill proved just as important as the new machines themselves. In a series of mills built between 1866 and 1879, Washburn lined up the machines in his plants close together in order to increase the speed of the process from beginning to end. As one journalist reported in 1886, "The manner in which the wheat, middlings, and flour circulate through the eight or nine stories, from side to side, from floor to floor, from machine to machine, nowhere needing the help of human hands, makes it seem like one vast living organism."[6] As a result of these processes, flour production in Minneapolis skyrocketed. By 1923 the milling process was almost entirely automated.

Large Minneapolis mills such as Washburn's benefited considerably from economies of scale. Large mills could easily borrow money to purchase the increasingly sophisticated milling machines. Large mills could afford to hire the best managers and workers to run those machines efficiently. Large mills could experiment with new machines because the older machines could still produce for them if something went wrong with a new one. And perhaps most importantly, large mills could secure better rates to store and transport wheat through volume discounts. Large mills could then serve greater numbers of customers.

Despite its technological sophistication, the Washburn mill still needed a considerable amount of labor to operate the machines, at least in the 1870s and 1880s. Indeed, the new process of milling required two extra steps, purifying and regrinding the middlings. By increasing the scale of the operation, the new mills transformed the task of milling. Where one person had done nearly everything, the process was now deeply divided. In the preindustrial era, a millwright decided the location of the mill along a river (since flour mills depended on water power for their energy). Then the millwright planned the dam, the mill, and machinery; cut down the wood to build the entire operation; and then supervised the construction and operation of the machinery. Such varied responsibilities are a sign of how small was the scale of these operations. No mill owner could do all of these things single handedly for a facility as large as the Washburn "A" Mill.

Once the flour milling process had been fully industrialized, the number of tasks necessary in the mill and the number of employees working there both jumped. As early as 1878 Minneapolis mills employed workers whose only job was to make sure that the machines worked properly: oilers who did nothing but oil the bearings, sweepers who only cleaned the floors, packers who did nothing but weigh and pack the flour, and nailers who did nothing but close and label the barrels of flour. Such an acute division of labor meant that Washburn and the other millers depended upon the skills of no one group of workers in order to operate their facilities (with the exception of one or two millwrights per plant). Since it was easy to train people to perform all of these tasks, the potential number of applicants for most jobs increased. This made it possible to hold down labor costs by paying workers lower wages.

Of course, Americans had begun moving west to set up farms long before the growth of these great flour mills. Still, the growth of these gigantic processors greatly affected the nature of farming in the upper Midwest. Minnesota proved a particularly good climate for winter wheat, a hard and hearty grain that could be turned into very fine white flour. As a result, almost every farmer in Minnesota came to grow this crop. Over time, many farms consolidated into giant "bonanza" farms that could get lower storage and freight rates thanks to their better bargaining position. To combat this kind of consolidation, flour producers joined together into a purchasing cartel in order to keep their costs down.

Before this late-stage industrialization, white flour had been universally associated with the diet of the rich because it was expensive to produce. Now these industrial processes changed white flour from an expensive commodity into an everyday item. People could get what they thought was a better-quality product for less money because giant mills could make mass quantities of it cheaply. (White flour was actually less nutritious since most of the nutrients in wheat come from the bran and the germ, either one of which makes flour brown.) Millers such as Washburn and Pillsbury paid for a direct railroad route from Minneapolis to the Great Lakes in order to get their product to market faster, thereby making their businesses at least partially vertically integrated. They also paid huge sums on advertising to establish their brands, thereby making the selling of the product easier.

Yet advertising could go only so far in developing a market. Thus, industrialization also led to the development of new markets for wheat overseas. Washburn pioneered the European flour trade in the late 1870s, precisely the same time that the gradual reduction process took hold in Minneapolis. European millers resisted American imports, fearing that they could not match the efficiencies of Washburn's and Pillsbury's production process. Therefore, these millers had to develop new domestic uses for their products. For example, excess production from the milling of all kinds of grains gave a strong impetus to the development of the modern breakfast cereal industry. In 1928 Washburn's firm (by then called the Washburn-Crosby Company) became the core of the new General Mills Corporation, a company that continues to dominate many fields of food production. Other companies that benefited from industrialization have not fared so well in recent times, often because of earlier struggles with their own employees.

Notes

1. Carroll D. Wright, "The Factory System as an Element in Civilization," *Journal of Social Science* 15 (February 1882): 102.

2. Andrew Carnegie, "The Gospel of Wealth," in *The Andrew Carnegie Reader*, ed. Joseph Frazier Wall (Pittsburgh: University of Pittsburgh Press, 1992), 131.

3. Carnegie, "An Employer's View of the Labor Question," in *The Andrew Carnegie Reader*, 96.

4. In Stephen Fraser, *Labor Will Rule: Sidney Hillman and the Rise of American Labor* (New York: Free Press, 1991), 28.

5. In *The Life Stories of Undistinguished Americans*, ed. Hamilton Holt (New York: James Pott & Co., 1906), 43.

6. Eugene V. Smalley, "The Flour Mills of Minneapolis," *The Century* 32 (May 1886): 42–43.

The Labor Question

Q. *How did workers respond to the difficult circumstances created by industrialization?*

In 1898 famed attorney Clarence Darrow defended Thomas I. Kidd, the general secretary of the Amalgamated Wood Workers Union, along with two members of that organization's local in Oshkosh, Wisconsin. The two rank-and-file woodworkers had been picket captains during an unsuccessful fourteen-week walkout for union recognition at the Paine Lumber Company. They and the leader of the national union that wanted to represent them were charged by the State of Wisconsin with conspiring to injure Paine Lumber's business by conducting a strike.

Darrow's strategy for the defense was to link the defendants to the most important social question of the day, "the labor question." As Darrow pointed out during his closing argument to the jury:

> On the one hand these powerful interests [meaning employers] are organized thoroughly, completely and they act together; and they turn to those poor slaves, whose liberty they take, and say to them, 'We will consult with you, but come alone to our office and then we will talk.' They say this because they wish to meet the weak and puny and helpless single individual with the great and powerful wealth and strength of their mighty corporations.[1]

The way for employees to solve this problem was obvious: to go into that office as a group and if they did not get what they wanted from their employer to go on strike as a group too. But how could they be sure this would work? After all, employers could usually find new workers, but employees who remained on strike for too long risked their livelihoods and even their lives. To win this case, Darrow was explaining to the jury how power was distributed in the workplace of the era of industrialization. Employers always had substantially more power than employees, unless those employees were highly skilled or had organized themselves into unions.

In 1883 the social theorist Henry George complained that industrialization degraded "men into the position of mere feeders of machines."[2] In truth, the feeders of machines were in some ways the lucky ones as the mechanization of different parts of production often meant that employers could lower their wage bills by mechanizing their operations and firing workers by the hundreds. Even those workers who remained employed despite the development of labor-saving technology still faced irregular employment, often because the factories where they worked shut down completely during off seasons. Since the labor pool for unskilled work was so large, these employers had complete confidence that they would find more than enough employees when they started up their factories again. "If a manager can secure men for $6 [a week] and pays more, he is stealing from the company," explained a stockholder in a Lawrence, Massachusetts, textile mill, one of the most mechanized industries in the country.[3] This attitude created an enormous impediment on the way up the socioeconomic ladder that many workers could not overcome.

Joining a trade union helped immeasurably when workers confronted their employers over life-or-death issues such as wages. The division of labor made many individual workers easily dispensable. The more people there were who could potentially do a job, the less an employer would have to pay to convince someone else to do it. Equally important, the drop in demand for skilled workers often led employers to make greater demands of the workers they did hire, such as extended hours. However, when workers banded together they could prevent such changes by shutting down production if they marched out in unison. American workers who were not union members inevitably suffered through the difficult circumstances that industrialization created because they thought they had no other choice. Workers in labor unions did not have it easy and did not win every battle with their employers, but at least they could fall back on their strength in numbers.

Therefore, most owners did everything they could to extinguish trade unions in America during this era in order to keep more of the profits created by industrialization for themselves. As a result of such policies, continual clashes between labor and management occurred in American industries of all kinds. Between the Great Railroad Strike of 1877 and the end of World War II in 1945, strikes were much more common than they are today. In fact, many of these conflicts were significant enough to threaten the entire American economy. While some of these strikes led to temporary victories for workers in certain industries, for the most part labor could not settle the labor question by itself. Other forces, in particular business and government, settled the labor question for them by preventing unions from forming. The federal and state governments used their military power against organized workers over and over again. Not until the 1930s would government play any positive part in the organizing activities of American labor.

Trade unions were not a panacea. In fact, unions often stood at the forefront of racist and anti-immigrant public policies. Understanding the general failure of the largest labor organizations of the day to ameliorate the negative effects of industrialization helps explain why it proceeded at a breakneck pace for so long. Workers, through their influence on the political system, could have been in a position to limit the damage that industrialization caused. They did not. Nevertheless, labor's critique of industrialization is important for understanding this phenomenon as a whole because it reads like a list of industrialization's worst effects. However, by offering this critique, unions got painted as impediments to progress. That was, in some way, the very reason for their existence. Some labor unions, however, served as a larger obstacle to industrial expansion than did others. How militant these organizations were was the most important factor in determining the size of the obstacle that they created. Each of the unions profiled below achieved limited success in shielding some of its members from the ill effects of industrialization, but none of them could prevent American businesses from dominating American economic life during this era.

The Knights of Labor

The Knights of Labor was the first successful national labor union formed to combat the accumulation of wealth that industrialization made possible. As one member of that organization described to a congressional committee investigating the labor question, "The men are looked upon as nothing more than parts of the machinery that they work. They are labeled and tagged, as the parts of a machine would be, and are only taken into account as a part of the machinery used for the profit of the manufacturer."[4] The Knights of Labor tried to serve as a counterweight to capital, which had grown stronger and richer because of industrialization. Sometimes the union actually succeeded, but it

The leadership of the Knights of Labor sought middle-class respectability, but their membership was radical enough that they quickly lost whatever respectability they had after the infamous Haymarket incident of 1886. *(Courtesy of the Library of Congress)*

could not sustain the level of success it achieved in its best years. The Knights included workers from all walks of life, everyone from farmers to glassblowers. In theory its potential members included everyone in society except a small minority of trades like doctors, politicians, and lawyers. Many of its members were skilled workers who already belonged to unions and who might be described as incipient members of the middle class.

The Knights of Labor began in Philadelphia in 1869 as a secret society of tailors who feared that knowledge of their union sympathies would lead their employers to fire them. The organization's initial leader was a tailor named Uriah Stephens, who decided to bring the group out into the open in 1878 in response to the partially successful nationwide railroad strike of 1877. Despite the best efforts of its skilled leadership, the Knights of Labor ran from the bottom up, not the top down. This was both its greatest strength and its greatest weakness. On one hand, strong local organizations were a major asset to the organization. As the constitution of the Knights explained, "The Local Assembly aims to assist members to better their condition, morally, socially and financially. It is a business firm, every member an equal partner, as much as a commercial house or a manufacturing establishment."[5] The shared culture of the Knights helped its members feel that they had allies in the struggle against industrialized capital. Union members took oaths and conducted rituals just as they did when it was a secret organization. These activities contributed to a spirit of solidarity that made it more likely that a member would stand by colleagues during adversity. These activities also took on the trappings of organized religion, therefore limiting the tensions that workers of different religions might have felt since they could all join this cause together. The culture of the Knights of Labor also served as a buffer against the prevalent anti-unionism of that era.

On the other hand, these kinds of democratically run organizations did not always make the best decisions, particularly over time as more unskilled workers entered the organization's ranks. Local assemblies of the Knights could be as small as ten workers and were free to change their district affiliations at will. This led to anarchy as locals tried to align with districts that agreed with their views. Most strikes waged by the Knights of Labor were instigated by local workers despite opposition from above. Stephens's successor, Terence Powderly, tried to teach his members other ways to settle differences with their employers besides going on strike. In 1881 the leadership even inserted a clause in the constitution demanding compulsory arbitration of disputes between labor and management. The strikes continued unabated.

This was not a problem for the organization early in the 1880s while it was still mostly winning its battles with management. The union's first important triumph was over Jay Gould's Western Union in 1883. Two years later the Knights of Labor proved that it was a force to be reckoned with in the American economy by winning a strike at Gould's Southwest Railroad. While railroads were always subject to strikes since they had so many skilled workers, this dispute was directed primarily at raising the wages of the less skilled. Although Gould refused to recognize the union, he did give the workers a raise. Fueled by such victories, the Knights claimed 500,000 members in 1886, the high point of its powers.[6] At least 65,000 of those members were women.[7]

Unfortunately, the union grew much too fast for its own good. For forty days in 1886, the organization refused to accept new membership applications because it could not process the ones it had. That same year, the Knights struck Gould's railroad again and lost. This was the defeat that first turned the public against the union. More importantly, when the leaders of the union quickly abandoned this second strike, many of the rank-and-file Knights abandoned them. After 1886 the total membership of the Knights declined sharply. The underlying reason for the organization's collapse can be found both in its own shortcomings and the public response to the Haymarket tragedy.

On May 1, 1886, thousands of Knights participated in nationwide rallies in support of the eight-hour day. Several days later, a group of Chicago anarchists organized a protest against violence during one of those eight-hour day strikes at a local agricultural implements producer. When the police tried to break up the demonstration in Chicago's Haymarket Square, an unknown assailant threw a bomb. Seven police officers died (mostly from their own bullets). Eight anarchists were charged with murder on the basis of their political beliefs. Even though the Knights of Labor had nothing to do with that incident, the union was caught up in a backlash against any organization or ideas that could be construed as radical. By 1893 the Knights had lost thousands of members and become only a shadow of its former organization.

Despite this collapse, the rise of the Knights of Labor spurred a much wider consideration of the labor question in all walks of American life. The relatively open shop committees that the group created, which often favored arbitration over striking, became the precedent for future experiments with industrial democracy. The Knights also definitively demonstrated that un-skilled workers could be organized, an issue that had been in doubt before that time. As industrialization progressed, this would become an increasingly important issue as less skilled workers rapidly proliferated. In fact, even skilled workers had trouble surviving during these difficult times.

The American Federation of Labor

Samuel Gompers, the first president of the American Federation of Labor (AFL), started his working life as a cigar roller. The changing conditions in that industry defined his labor philosophy and the way that he and his organization responded to industrialization. Cigar making required considerable skill. As the economist Edith Abbott observed: "No part of the making of cigars is heavy work, nor does it, like the manufacture of clothing, require great endurance. Skill depends upon manual dexterity, upon delicacy and sensitiveness of touch."[8] While there were machines that made cigars, they could not increase the output of ordinary labor by more than 50 percent, and a really good roller could match the machine in output. The real benefit of these machines came from replacing skilled workers like Gompers with young girls who acted as machine tenders. The company's profit came not from increased output, but from decreasing labor costs. This explains why cigar workers' unions fought hard against mechanization. What saved them is that the machine-made cigars were inferior to the ones that skilled workers made by hand. Therefore, the industry could never be fully feminized or industrialized. This meant that Gompers's union, the Cigar Makers International Union, by and large successfully resisted the changes that industrialization wrought.

Despite its success, the cigar makers' union did not stick its collective head in the sand and wait for industrialization to run its course. In the late 1870s it reorganized itself to gain greater staying power. It raised dues and initiation fees in order to fatten its treasury in case of strikes. It began to equalize funds across locals so that strong locals could help weak ones survive. Other unions of skilled workers in different industries began to copy these tactics, and before long these business unions tried to join together into a national coalition. Earlier efforts along these lines had collapsed, but now the ill effects of industrialization served as the glue to hold skilled workers together. After all, employers organized into national trade associations. Why shouldn't workers organize into national unions in order to meet the power of organized business head on?

In 1881 Gompers and others organized the Federation of Organized Trades and Labor Unions of the United States and Canada. It quickly failed—largely because members of the Knights of Labor withdrew from the organization shortly after its first convention for fear that this federation would compete for the allegiance of its most skilled members. In 1886, however, skilled workers like Gompers formed the AFL, and that organization has lasted down to this day. The AFL was not a trade union but an umbrella organization that included unions mostly consisting of skilled workers from all kinds of trades. These unions had autonomy on matters relating to their own industry, but the AFL gave them a chance to act together for the benefit of working men as a whole. However, since most of the unions it included had skilled workers for members, the AFL membership was largely white and native born. In other words, it was hardly a representative cross-section of the American working class. This would prove to be one of its greatest weaknesses.

Another important reason that the AFL survived industrialization was Gompers's insistence that, like the Cigar Makers International Union, AFL member unions work toward establishing permanent organizations. Perhaps the most important element that ensured the AFL's survival was its conservative philosophy. As Gompers explained it, "Unions pure and simple are the natural organization of wage workers to secure their present and practical improvement and to achieve their final emancipation."[9] What did "pure and simple" unionism mean? It meant raising wages, improving working conditions and benefits, and nothing else. Like the leadership of the Knights, Gompers did not favor strikes, but he did lead them when necessary. He had to, living at a time when unions had such fierce enemies. However, Gompers preferred accommodation to confrontation. He sought agreements that allowed employers to make profits in their operations so they could split those proceeds with their workers. Many unions within the AFL backed different approaches than did Gompers. Most notably, Gompers struggled mightily with socialists in the federation's ranks throughout his long presidency. In general, though, the organization remained extremely conservative.

Despite its conservatism, the existence of the AFL still created a fierce backlash among employers against its member unions. While Gompers tried to find common ground with some employers willing to talk to him, the National Association of Manufacturers (NAM) sought to destroy the AFL entirely. In 1906 the AFL had called for a boycott of Buck's Stove and Range Company because of its antiunion labor policies. Its president, who was also president of the NAM, sued and got a sweeping court injunction banning the boycott. When Gompers and two other AFL leaders refused to obey the injunction, they were sentenced to prison for contempt. Only a United States Supreme Court decision declaring the issue moot saved Gompers from incarceration. Gompers's decision to participate in the management of World War I by taking an advisory post with the Wilson administration helped give his organization legitimacy and public acceptance, even during the generally antiunion decade of the 1920s.

Other than its embrace of "pure and simple unionism," the best indication of the AFL's conservatism was the long struggle between Gompers and the socialists in the ranks of its member unions. Socialists supported the merger of the political and economic ends of trade unionism. Unions, in other words, would have been the vehicle for achieving their revolution. Gompers took a much more practical approach. "It is ridiculous to imagine," he argued, "that the wage-workers can be slaves in employment yet achieve control of the polls. There never yet existed coincident with each other autocracy in the shop and democracy in political life."[10] The problem with this approach was that it allowed only a limited number of workers to achieve the protection from the ravages of industrialization that the trade unions in the AFL provided.

The AFL still exists today as a component part of the AFL-CIO (Congress of Industrial Organizations), the largest labor federation in the country. Despite its survival, the AFL never represented more than 5 percent of the American workforce during the era of industrialization. It had no money or personnel to organize the unorganized and even if it had, it would not have targeted unskilled workers for organization. They were too poor and too hard to control to be an asset to the AFL's member unions. Besides, many of those at the bottom of the economic ladder were immigrants or African Americans. By then, employers had decades of practice dividing workers by race and ethnicity so that industrialized production could continue unabated. Unskilled workers needed a union champion of their own.

The Industrial Workers of the World

While the AFL's motto was "A fair day's wage for a fair day's work," the Industrial Workers of the World (IWW or Wobblies) called for "abolition of the wage system."[11] This union of the downtrodden began in 1905 in

Chicago at a convention full of famous labor radicals like Eugene V. Debs and Mary Jones (better known as "Mother" Jones). At least one attendee was a spy sent not by an employer organization, but by Samuel Gompers; conservative trade unions were as much an enemy to the IWW as was management. The creation of the IWW was a direct response to the difficulties created by industrialization. As the text of an early IWW ritual outlined, "The inventions and improvements in machinery and the consequent displacement of labor make it imperative that we should unite for our own protection, for the protection of our homes and those who are dear to us as life itself."[12] Unfortunately for the workers it wanted to organize, the IWW had no centralized organization and no leadership with operational control of its activities. In fact, the Wobblies had no single leader to administer the organization at all. Leaders went to strikes after they broke out, not before, to help organize. This often led to chaos at the site of a dispute, but many radicals in the IWW preferred chaos to any hint of compromise with authority, even the authority of their own organization. As a result of its unpredictable, bottom-up organization, the IWW never became a significant force in the American economy.

What really worried Gompers and the industrialists was not the absolute number of Wobblies (there were probably never more than 50,000 of them nationwide), but their potential for making trouble. The IWW was more of an offensive than a defensive union. While union representatives sometimes got summoned to places where trouble had already begun, roving bands of organizers usually started their own trouble. The famous Lawrence, Massachusetts, textile strike of 1912, for instance, was largely inspired by the work of an itinerant twenty-six-year old Wobbly agitator named Joseph Ettor. A small strike at one mill that had been called the previous spring had petered out. Ettor was called back to Lawrence by local organizers specifically to provide the inspiration to reignite it. "The Industrial Workers was a radical organization," a local strike leader later remembered. "For my part, I didn't care what they were. I was looking for the organizer of the strike."[13] Workers who were satisfied with the benefits that industrialization offered them were willing to accept the difficult working conditions that this process produced. Workers who were unhappy with those conditions were willing to align themselves with any organization that they thought was on their side.

The IWW specifically looked for the most alienated workers possible as the main source for its members. These were the unskilled, people who had suffered most from industrialization since they were the easiest to replace: migrant farmhands displaced by new farm machinery, immigrants in textile mills with no funds to return home, timber workers in isolated camps who held perhaps the most dangerous jobs in America. Their employers assumed that these workers would be desperate because they needed their jobs to survive. The IWW proved otherwise. Many of the workers who struck under the IWW banner were immigrants whose home countries had much stronger radical traditions than did America. Wobblies were not really a threat to the established order, but the union's politics were radical enough that employers and governments alike tended to magnify the threat posed by the organization well out of proportion to what the Wobblies were capable of accomplishing.

Oftentimes the IWW's politics were so distasteful, particularly to skilled workers, that employers could count on other workers to beat the IWW for them. Consider the strike at the Pressed Steel Car Company of McKees Rocks, Pennsylvania, in 1909. It started in the riveting department, where semiskilled men assembled railway cars, because the workers did not understand the system by which they got their wages. Two years earlier, management had instituted a piece rate system for determining wages along with a new assembly line production method that—although not as complete as the one Ford created later—still significantly quickened the pace of work. In other words, thanks to industrialization, employees had to work harder to get paid the same because they were now paid by output rather than by the hour. The wages of most workers, particularly the unskilled immigrants, decreased considerably as a result. Both skilled and unskilled workers initially joined the strike called in order to protest this situation. The unskilled workers, however, called in the IWW to help protect their interests when the skilled workers called for a hasty settlement.

Playing off the skilled, native-born American workers against the less-skilled immigrants became the most effective weapon the Pressed Steel Car Company had to win the dispute. Under fear of violence, the company chose a few carefully screened workers to announce a second settlement that the IWW initially applauded. Unfortunately, the concessions that management made to unskilled workers had no teeth behind them. When the IWW leaders realized that they had been deceived, they tried to restart the conflict. At that point, the skilled worker who had once led the strike filed a complaint to get the local Wobbly leader arrested. Upon his arrest, the strike fizzled completely. After the strike, management was delighted to deal with the skilled workers' organization precisely because it was not the

The Industrial Workers of the World offered a scathing class-based critique of America's industrial society. That explains why the powers of the state eventually all but destroyed this radical labor organization.

IWW. In a way, then, the strike was a victory, but not for IWW members. This story exemplifies how radical organizations can help bring about marginal improvements for workers, but the unskilled workers whom the IWW best represented were not the main beneficiaries. The workers who needed the most help still were not happy.

The unwanted attention of the federal government was largely responsible for the IWW's effective demise. The Wobblies were fierce opponents of World War I. In 1916 the union passed a resolution at its convention to that effect, even before the United States entered the war. This declaration alone was enough to make the *New York Times* and other respectable newspapers call for the union to be suppressed, which the government did in September 1917. That is when the Department of Justice raided forty-eight IWW meeting halls across the country and arrested 165 Wobbly leaders for violating the Espionage Act, a new law designed to limit opposition to the war. Each prisoner was convicted. The organization's most important leader, William "Big Bill" Haywood, fled to Russia in order to escape jail. While the IWW survived (most notably to lead a strike in the Colorado coal fields in 1927), the organization was never as strong as it was before the raids.

The fate of the IWW during the war greatly affected the fate of labor unions of all kinds. The existence of these apparently un-American radicals gave employers a very broad brush with which they could paint organized labor in general. The National Association of Manufacturers, for example, directly equated all trade unions with Bolshevism, the communist faction in Russia that took power in 1917. The steel industry used the IWW and the communist affiliation of William Z. Foster, who led the union organizing drive there during the war, to delegitimize the strike it faced in 1919, after the government stopped enforcing labor peace in all vital war industries. As a result, most workers during the 1920s had to face the perils of industrialization without the help of union representation. Determined to keep as much of the benefits of industrialization to themselves as they could, managers fought off labor organizations of all kinds even after Franklin D. Roosevelt's New Deal gave unions the legal legitimacy they had lacked during earlier decades. By that time, the first generation of eastern and southern European immigrants who had needed trade unions the most yet did not have them had retired or died. Their struggle went far beyond simply economic discrimination.

Notes

1. *Clarence Darrow, Attorney for the Damned*, ed. Arthur Weisberg (New York: Simon & Schuster, 1959), 286.

2. In Alan Trachtenberg, *The Incorporation of America: Culture and Society in the Gilded Age* (New York: Hill & Wang, 2007), 43.

3. In Nell Irvin Painter, *Standing at Armageddon: The United States, 1877–1919* (New York: W.W. Norton, 1987), xxxvi.

4. In Painter, xxxv.

5. In Carroll D. Wright, "Historical Sketch of the Knights of Labor," *Quarterly Journal of Economics* 1 (January 1887): 160.

6. Wright, 156.

7. Lara Vapnek, *Breadwinners: Working Women and Economic Independence, 1865–1920* (Urbana: University of Illinois Press, 2009), 43.

8. Edith Abbott, *Women in Industry: A Study in American Economic History* (New York: D. Appleton & Company, 1910), 186–187.

9. In Trachtenberg, 95.

10. Samuel Gompers, *Labor and the Common Welfare* (New York: E.P. Dutton, 1919), 125.

11. In William M. Adler, *The Man Who Never Died: The Life, Times, and Legacy of Joe Hill, American Labor Icon* (New York: Bloomsbury, 2011), 10.

12. Jim Crutchfield's IWW Page, "Ritual of the Industrial Workers of the World," Chicago, July 7, 1905, www.workerseducation.org/crutch/constitution/ritual.html.

13. In Bruce Watson, *Bread & Roses: Mills, Migrants and the Struggle for the American Dream* (New York: Penguin, 2005), 50.

Immigration

Q. *Why did America restrict access to*
some immigrants and not others?

In 1889 Jane Addams and her friend Ellen Gates Starr opened Hull House in an immigrant neighborhood on the west side of Chicago. Hull House was a settlement house, a model for middle-class women helping the poor. These kinds of houses had originated in England a few years earlier. Based on that English example, Addams wanted to help people who had trouble coping with the many economic changes created by industrialization that affected their lives and livelihoods. Most of those people were immigrants. In order to help them fit into American society, Addams wanted them to understand how the American economy worked and where they fit into the larger picture of industrialization.

As part of their introduction to life in America, Addams showed the mostly female workers who took advantage of the Hull House programs the role they played in mass production. "[If] she understands the design she is elaborating in its historic relation to art and decoration," wrote Addams, "her daily life is lifted from drudgery to one of self-conscious activity, and her pleasure and intelligence is registered in her product."[1] Addams believed that immigrants, through their experiences in their home countries, had much to offer American society. Like the English language classes and housekeeping lessons for which Hull House is now best remembered, industrial education facilitated a similar kind of assimilation that America's many immigrants desperately needed.

The late nineteenth and early twentieth centuries were the heyday of both industrialization and immigration in the United States. The total number of immigrants admitted to America increased from 457,257 in 1880 to 1,218,480 in 1914. The greatest spike in the number of immigrants came between 1900 and 1910, when the yearly total of immigrants surpassed a million four times.[2] Economic forces go far to explain why many immigrants came to America. Even immigrants who left their homelands primarily to escape religious persecution stood to benefit economically from their displacement. Economic forces also explain why corporations wanted immigrants to enter the country. Cheap labor allowed factory owners to keep more profits from industrialization for themselves. Less obvious is why so many native-born Americans wanted to keep many of those immigrants out. In this instance, economic forces interacted with racism. Underlying this tug of war were the changes in the overall economy that industrialization wrought.

Unlike native-born workers, immigrants gladly accepted difficult and tedious industrial jobs because of their desire for the money and the improvement in the quality of life (at least compared to that in their home countries) that came with them. Some, like thirty-three-year-old carpenter Johann Tyni, did not thrive in this environment. "I work too hard and I am all played out," he admitted in 1912, just three years after his arrival. "I am downhearted all the time and the thoughts make me cry."[3] Others thrived, becoming the ancestors of many Americans today. While it is impossible to determine the exact success rate of new immigrants, the huge pool of immigrants arriving in the United States during this era meant there were very many of both. Improvements in steamships that carried immigrants to the United States from all over the world and the growth of the railroad system that delivered new arrivals to where the jobs were ensured that employers had more than enough labor to keep their mines, mills, and manufacturing plants running smoothly.

From a manager's standpoint, immigrant labor was often ideal. Since many immigrants performed only unskilled labor, they were both cheap and easy to replace. Since machines did much of the work in the modern factory, workers required little training. Many immigrants did not even need to speak English to work in a modern factory. They learned everything about their job and communicated with their bosses through hand signals. If particular immigrants failed at work or quit, they could always be replaced by new immigrants. This came in very handy if those long-time workers wanted a raise or tried to organize a union. Employers also liked the fact that the language barrier between immigrant groups usually kept workers from organizing together. Sometimes long-standing ethnic tensions left over from the Old World hindered organization too.

Old-stock Americans who did not become capitalists, or even middle managers, often blamed immigrants for their plight, especially as the number of immigrants to the United States increased over time. Thanks to the willingness of many newly arrived workers to accept less in wages than what was necessary to achieve what was already known as the American standard of living, immigration had negative economic effects on some native-born Americans, such as lower wages in some industries. Furthermore, by working long hours, immigrant workers increased pressure on native-born Americans to work longer hours too. These effects were an important reason why many of the people already in the United States came to support immigration restriction legislation. After all, it seemed easier to stop immigration than to stop industrialization, a phenomenon that few people understand even many years later.

Yet despite economic fears, most immigration restriction proponents did not favor a blanket ban on the arrival of new workers. Immigration to America was never completely restricted. Most immigration reformers merely wanted to regulate immigration in order to improve the quality of the newly emerging industrial society. Educating immigrant workers about what their employers expected of them was one way for that to happen. However, there was a sizable number of nativists who wanted to restrict the admission of immigrants based upon their perceived racial inferiority, particularly after the turn of the twentieth century. These nativists wanted to keep some races and classes of workers out of the country. Yet even nonwhite immigrants were not subject to complete restriction, at least at first.

The Chinese Exclusion Act

It was no coincidence that the first people restricted from entering the United States all had the same skin color and that the color of their skin was not white. Chinese immigrants were singled out for harsh treatment because they were easier to identify by sight than any previous immigrant group. Yet if skin color alone were enough motivation for immigration restriction in this instance, why were not other minority racial groups also banned from entry into the United States? In 1880, in the last census before they were officially excluded, people of Chinese descent constituted only .002 percent of the American population.[4] How could so few people threaten every native-born worker in America?

The reason the Chinese got singled out lies in the text of the Chinese Exclusion Act of 1882. The law begins by stating that "the coming of Chinese laborers to this country endangers the good order of certain localities."[5] Indeed, the law repeatedly stresses that it applies not to Chinese people in general but only to Chinese laborers because of the economic

Chinese immigration became a political issue for economic reasons as well as for racial reasons. *(Courtesy of the Library of Congress)*

competition they offered to native-born Americans. While undoubtedly racist legislation, the Chinese Exclusion Act of 1882 was couched entirely in economic terms. The so-called Gentleman's Agreement of 1907, which excluded a large segment of Japanese workers from the United States, worked similarly. "Gentlemen" could still enter the country, but not working-class Japanese.

Only in 1888 was the law broadened to apply to every Chinese person, worker or otherwise. This happened because this small minority came to represent the economic threat that competition for jobs posed to all working-class people. Even regions that had few Chinese workers became centers of anti-Chinese prejudice because workers feared that the economic conditions of the Chinese would become the norm in industrialized America whether Chinese people were present there or not. The Chinese were the typical native-born American's worst nightmare both economically and culturally, and a nightmare does not have to be real in order to be frightening. Even if no Chinese lived near you, competition with them could bring you down to their economic level.

The fact that Chinese immigrants were concentrated on the West Coast did not help their economic condition. Chinese immigrants had first arrived in California as part of the 1849 California Gold Rush. More came to work on the Central Pacific Railway, part of the famous transcontinental railroad. Here they did the most dangerous work, like blasting mountain passes open. The president of the Central Pacific, Charles Crocker, deliberately sought out Chinese workers once they had demonstrated their worth. Those workers were not, however, rewarded for their service to the company. "After we got Chinamen to work," he noted, "we took the more intelligent of the white laborers and made foremen of them. I know of several of them now who never expected, never had a dream that they were going to be anything but shovelers of dirt, hewers of wood and drawers of water, and they are now respectable farmers, owning farms."[6] Whites who did not become managers came to identify Chinese labor with increased management control because if white workers would not submit to that kind of authority they could presumably be replaced by Chinese workers who would. In fact, that is precisely what happened in California agriculture.

Starting in the 1870s, after the transcontinental railroad was completed, Chinese workers began working in vineyards, orchards, and fields around California. They quickly gained a reputation for industriousness and willingness to labor under the worst of conditions. As their numbers grew, many Chinese workers signed on with labor bosses who would send them to do major harvesting or reclamation projects throughout California. The great irony of Chinese exclusion was that the United States was experiencing a labor shortage in the years preceding the passage of the act. In other words, there was more than enough work to go around for both white and Chinese laborers, even in California. Unfortunately for everyone involved, white workers tended to think otherwise. They were looking for scapegoats, and the Chinese served that role well.

When this very visible minority started taking jobs that had previously gone to native-born Americans, violence ensued. In 1877, for example, whites murdered four Chinese field hands in their bunkhouse west of Chico. That was just one incident in a wave of violence against Chinese workers in the years preceding the passage of the exclusion law. Sometimes this anger was directed against employers who hired

Chinese workers instead. In some cases, former Chinese field hands or labor bosses went into business for themselves and became farmers. Just as when panning for gold, if you could produce a crop, the color of your skin did not matter. People would still buy your commodity. It was precisely the economic success of Chinese laborers that led to calls for their exclusion, especially on the West Coast and among labor unions whose mostly white members feared competing against them. It did not help that the Chinese had a reputation for working harder than Americans. Preventing that ethic from becoming the expected norm for agricultural work made economic sense. The Chinese were economically threatening when they were downtrodden. They were economically threatening when they were successful. They simply could not win in a society dominated by white, native-born Americans.

The common white fear of a "yellow horde" did nothing to help the Chinese out of this difficult population. The Chinese population of the United States could not expand on its own because it was over-whelmingly male, since Chinese culture generally prevented women from emigrating. Therefore, this tiny racial minority would have had a hard time establishing a foothold among the white population even if immigration had not been restricted. Other changes, most notably the industrialization of agriculture in California (where the Chinese did have a foothold), had much more significant effects on the working conditions of native-born Americans. That kind of change, however, was much harder for politicians to legislate against or for ordinary workers to control in any manner.

Despite being excluded, the Chinese laborers who entered the country before the law took effect still left a mark on California's agriculture long after workers of other nationalities replaced them in the fields. Chinese laborers dug irrigation canals, cleared brush, picked fruit, and did many other tasks that helped establish agriculture as California's largest industry. The growers who hired them also established a labor pattern that has persisted for decades. Growers had to go through labor contractors who would divide their workforce, often on the basis of skill, and rent their services to a grower who did not have enough workers for a limited period such as harvest time, when more labor was needed than at any other point during the year. The way growers used Chinese labor, dividing them extensively by task, came to set the pattern that remains in the agricultural industry down to this day. After the turn of the century, Japanese workers and later Mexican workers replaced the

Chinese in the fields. Nevertheless, the way that large farmers used farm labor stayed the same. The division of labor quickly became standard practice on farms throughout the country. "Conscientious effort should at all times be made to place a man where he can work to the best advantage," wrote the author of a textbook called *Farm Management* in 1921. "It is better to make each man responsible for certain duties than to use men indiscriminately for all kinds of work."[7] Only small family farmers undertook a variety of tasks because they did not have enough workers to divide. The efficiencies of the division of labor and the increasing mechanization of the industry together explain the growth of large farms at the expense of family farms for all crops in California during the era of industrialization and beyond.

The Alien Contract Labor Law and Other Immigration Regulation

The underpinnings of the Chinese Exclusion Act revealed economic anxieties. So did the many less important immigration restrictions implemented between 1882 and 1917. Most immigrants to the United States faced none of these restrictions, but the difference between those who did and those who did not reveals a great deal about what concerned Americans at this time. Many of these restrictions were geared toward limiting immigration to those newcomers who were strong and thus capable of working in the factories and mines where their labor was desperately needed. If they could not contribute to the economy, they were, at least theoretically, kept out of the country so they would not have to fall back upon the limited number of public charities that offered the only safety net before the advent of the federal welfare system during the 1930s. The goal of immigration regulation was—as a doctor at the immigration station on Ellis Island in New York Harbor put it in 1903—to serve "as a sieve fine enough in the mesh to keep out the diseased, the pauper and the criminal while admitting the immigrant with two strong arms, a sound body and a stout heart."[8] That mesh was designed to block potential immigrants on both economic and racial grounds.

While the Chinese Exclusion Act passed for both economic and racial reasons, there were plenty of restrictions on immigration passed during this era for purely economic reasons. The United States passed its first alien contract labor law in 1885. It outlawed the recruitment and prepayment for the transportation of foreign citizens to work in the United

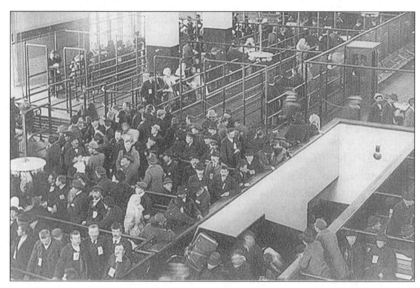

Immigrants coming to America through Ellis Island were inspected to determine not just their fitness to become Americans, but also their fitness to become productive members of an industrial society. *(Courtesy of the Library of Congress)*

States. Skilled workers, actors, singers—even domestic servants—were exempt since the express purpose of the act was to protect American workers from having to compete against immigrants who might have been recruited to fill their jobs at a lower wage. These restrictions and their enforcement only tightened over time. By 1911 a congressional committee investigating the contract labor issue concluded, "It is difficult . . . to conceive how the letter of the law respecting the importation of contract labor could be made more stringent than at present."[9] Yet despite such legislation, employers and immigrants could evade these restrictions easily. The benefits of industrialization gave them ample incentive to do so. Employers got to hire comparatively cheap labor, while immigrants often made more in wages than they ever could have hoped to earn in their largely nonindustrialized homelands.

This explains why countless Europeans were more than willing to immigrate to the United States without having jobs lined up in advance of their departure, and why many American employers were more than happy to hire them. Italians, for example, were "constantly bestirring others to go," expounded one government report. "Each Italian in the United States can easily secure a place for a friend and the process is repeated."[10] If they did not make use of such networks, employers could easily get around the contract labor laws by offering verbal assurances of employment and instructing immigrants not to tell immigration inspectors about these arrangements. Stories about the terrific economic conditions in America passed on by already arrived immigrants also explain why immigrants took the risk of emigrating.

The exact process through which members of different immigrant groups arrived in America and found work varied. Many Greeks and Italians, for example, came as a result of the padrone system. This was a network of labor agents who paid for the passage of immigrants in exchange for working in particular jobs upon arrival. Many of these jobs required hard labor. Quickly recognizing that they were free to move as they wished in the United States, many workers who arrived under this or similar systems never arrived at their appointed places of employment and went off somewhere else in order to work for themselves. In short, they quickly took to the free enterprise system and sold their labor to the highest bidder.

Fearing that their members would be displaced by this comparatively cheap labor, trade unions were a driving force behind the alien contract labor laws and other forms of immigration restriction. European immigrants offered the same potential competition for jobs that the Chinese had, and Europeans came to the United States in far greater numbers. Faced with this threat to the livelihood of its members, even the leader of an inclusive organization like Terence Powderly of the Knights of Labor spoke out against the tide of immigrants. "The steamship dumps its human freight on our shores and takes its profits," he wrote in his autobiography; "the corporation reaps the benefit of the immigrants' presence by having its labor performed for half nothing; the poor immigrant lives but twenty-four hours ahead of the poorhouse, [and] the man he displaces becomes a tramp."[11] Native-born Americans wanted better for themselves, and trade unions purported to want better for everyone.

This kind of economic justification for immigration restriction illustrated a real problem. Mechanization turned many manufacturing jobs into nothing but machine tending, which made workers largely interchangeable. The more workers available to perform this less-skilled labor, the lower they would be paid, whether immigrant or native-born. Industrialization had made it easier than ever to hire untrained workers, and immigrants offered employers a huge pool of new workers to train. Two prominent economists explained the problem this way in an anti-immigration tract from 1912: "A large number of illustrations of this tendency might be cited. Probably three of the best, however, are the automatic looms and ring spindles in the cotton-goods manufacturing industry, the bottle-blowing and casting machines in bottle and other glass factories, and the machines for mining coal."[12] Skilled workers had to compete against both immigrants and machines. Therefore, their pay generally dropped whether their jobs got mechanized or not. Furthermore, with an increased pool of workers to choose from, employers often demanded that their employees work longer hours because they knew that desperate immigrants would accept whatever terms of employment they could get. Desperate native-born Americans had to accept such terms too or risk permanent structural unemployment. The old jobs that once ensured them a comfortable standard of living were gradually disappearing.

The Dillingham Commission

It seems logical to think that anti-immigrant sentiment was primarily a social and cultural phenomenon. Immigration restriction proponents often depicted the supposed inferiority of immigrants in starkly racial terms. Many immigrants, especially second-generation immigrants, used the products of industrialization to blend in with other Americans in the hopes that prejudice against them might dissipate somehow. Instead, opposition to immigration tended to escalate as the number of immigrants coming to America increased. This suggests that there was an important economic dimension to anti-immigration sentiment too. In 1894 a main force in the anti-immigrant movement, the Immigration Restriction League, explained it this way: "The protection which an American workingman needs is against those classes of workers who come here with lower standards, lower aims, lower desires and lower morals." The league wanted a fair economic fight, and in the economic battle between immigrants and native-born workers the willingness of immigrants to accept less was their greatest strength. "The competition of his equals need not and ought not to be feared," the organization wrote, "but the unlimited freedom of immigration of other classes, now allowed, tends to depress wages, and degrade the high standards of living and character of the American citizen."[13] "Equals" meant people of the same or similar race, but the economic effects of immigration awakened racist sentiments among many.

This tendency is well illustrated by the work of the United States Immigration Commission, nicknamed after its leader, Senator William Dillingham of Vermont. The Dillingham Commission operated from 1907 to 1911. Its final report stretched to forty-one volumes at just under 41,000 pages. Its studies offered considerable data for immigration restriction proponents and opponents alike. However, the commission ultimately concluded that immigration was primarily an economic issue. Its main policy recommendation was a literacy test that required reading forty words from the Bible in the immigrant's native tongue. Such a law was not to be implemented until 1917. Even then, few people were barred from entering the United States by failing the literacy test during its first five years in effect. In real terms, then, the impact of the Dillingham Commission was minimal.

In historical terms, though, the work of the Dillingham Commission helped clarify how immigration had changed in the decades preceding the issuance of its reports. The commission was the first organization to recognize that the point of origin of immigration to the United States had changed around 1880. Before that year, most European immigrants had come from the northern and western part of Europe. After 1880 most immigrants came from southern and eastern Europe. Not coincidently, this was about the time when American industrialization greatly accelerated. The commission also argued that most of the immigrants who arrived after 1880 were racially inferior to those who came before. Therefore, it argued that further immigration from those points of origin should be significantly reduced.

Despite some excellent research, a few investigators working for the Dillingham Commission dealt in the worst kinds of scientific racism prevalent during this era. For example, the commission hired the famous anthropologist Franz Boas to measure the skulls of immigrants and their children in order to judge the physical changes brought on by the American environment. The use of head size as an indicator of racial quality dated back to 1842, but the success of William Z. Ripley's *The Races of Europe*, first published in 1899, gave this particular pseudoscience a new life. Ripley called cephalic indexes, as the scales used to measure heads were known, "one of the best available tests of race known."[14] In order to keep the so-called inferior races out of the country and let the so-called superior races into the country, such schemes seemed to make sense at the time. Boas actually concluded that the cranial capacity of immigrants grew in the American environment, implying that even those people with smaller skulls could make it in America, but the commission still came out for limited immigration restriction because of the importance it attributed to economic concerns.

When it came to those economic concerns, the Dillingham Commission did not pull its punches. "Further general legislation concerning the admission of aliens should be based primarily upon economic or business considerations," concluded the commission report.[15] That perspective is clearly visible in the commission's many other reports on immigrants in industries around the country. According to another commission report, for example, the numbers of immigrants "are so great and the influx is so continuous that even with the remarkable expansion of industry during the past few years there has been created an oversupply of unskilled labor."[16] The effects of that oversupply, the commission explained, were clearly visible: "While it may not have lowered in a marked degree the American standard of living, it has introduced a lower standard which has become prevalent in the unskilled industry at large."[17] Industrialization, by deskilling particular jobs, made this influx possible. Do the same thing over and over each day and you do not even have to be able to converse with your fellow workers in order to get the job done. In fact, the quieter most workers were, the more their bosses liked it. This not only meant that workers were not organizing; it meant that they were paying more attention to production.

Immigration to America first began to wane with the outbreak of World War I. That conflict made it nearly impossible for anyone to leave Europe. Nevertheless, lobbying for immigration restriction continued. In fact, fears about whether immigrants really supported America during the war actually strengthened the call for the kinds of immigration restriction championed by the Dillingham Commission. During the 1920s, the commission's work served as justification for a series of laws designed to restrict immigration. The first immigration restrictions of the decade passed in 1921, creating a quota of 3 percent of the existing population in America from any European country ten years earlier as the limit on the number of immigrants who could be admitted in that year. The most significant of these laws was the Johnson-Reed Act of 1924, which cut the quotas even further and gave an advantage to the northern and western European immigrants whom the racists favored. The allowable number of immigrants from Italy, for example, decreased from 40,000 a year to just 3,845. Nevertheless, 287,000 immigrants per year were still allowed after these restrictions were in place, thereby demonstrating that labor needs still existed.[18]

But with many fewer Europeans to employ in their factories, business owners looked to the south and the southwest in order to meet their needs for unskilled labor. Immigration quotas did not apply to countries in the Western Hemisphere. As result, Hispanic immigration into the United States increased sharply in response to these restrictions. So did the number of African Americans who left the South in the hopes of a better life. Many of these new immigrants, just like the immigrants of an earlier era, came to live in the northern cities that housed most of the factories where industrialization took place.

Notes

1. In Jackson Lears, *No Place of Grace: Antimodernism and the Transformation of American Culture, 1880–1920* (New York: Pantheon, 1981), 79.
2. In Edwin W. Bowen, "Immigration (1789–1916)," *Encyclopedia Americana* (New York: Encyclopedia Americana Corporation, 1920), 27:483.
3. In Vincent J. Cannato, *American Passage: The History of Ellis Island* (New York: HarperCollins, 2009), 1.
4. From Ronald Takaki, *Strangers From a Different Shore: A History of Asian Americans*, rev. ed. (New York: Back Bay, 1998), 110.
5. National Archives, "Chinese Exclusion Act," Our Documents, www.ourdocuments.gov/doc.php?flash=true&doc=47.
6. In Ronald Takaki, *Iron Cages: Race and Culture in Nineteenth Century America* (New York: Oxford University Press, 1990), 238.
7. R.L. Adams, *Farm Management: A Text-book for Student, Investigator, and Investor* (New York: McGraw Hill, 1921), 545.
8. In Cannato, 57.
9. United States Immigration Commission, *Abstracts of the Reports of the Immigration Commission* (Washington, DC: Government Printing Office, 1911), 2:380.
10. In Cannato, 67.
11. Terence Powderly, *The Path I Trod: Autobiography of Terence Powderly*, ed. Harry J. Carman et al. (New York: Columbia University Press, 1940), 410.
12. Jeremiah W. Jenks and W. Jett Lauck, *The Immigration Problem: A Study of American Immigration*, 2nd ed. (New York: Funk and Wagnall's, 1912), 187.
13. Immigration Restriction League, "Twenty Reasons Why Immigration Should Be Further Restricted Now," 1894, http://pds.lib.harvard.edu/pds/view/6523551.
14. In Nell Irvin Painter, *The History of White People* (New York: W.W. Norton, 2010), 215.
15. United States Immigration Commission, *Abstracts*, 1:45.
16. In United States Immigration Commission, "Immigration of Aliens Into the United States," Report No. 149, 63d Congress, 2d session, 4.
17. United States Immigration Commission, Abstracts, 1:39.
18. Cannato, 341.

Urbanization

Q. Where will all the new workers live?

Industrialization spurred the growth of cities in America. Between 1850 and 1900, the population of New York City grew from approximately half a million to about 3.5 million people. Philadelphia grew from a little more than 100,000 people in 1850 to over 1.2 million people in 1900. In 1900 Chicago had just shy of 1.7 million people. It had been nothing but a village in 1850.[1] In fact, during this period Chicago was the fastest-growing city in the entire world. City leaders were so confident of continued growth that they built streetcar lines into cornfields. Overall, the total percentage of Americans who lived in cities increased from 15.3 percent in 1850 to 39.7 percent in 1900. In 1920 the Census Bureau found for the first time that the majority of Americans lived in cities.[2] Much of this urban growth came as a result of immigration from abroad. However, internal migration also fueled the growth of cities. People moved from the countryside to the cities because that is where the jobs were in this changing economy.

Urban growth can serve as a proxy for industrialization. Factories were concentrated in urban areas during this era. In order to understand this, it helps to remember that a factory need not be located in a large building. The principles behind industrialization could turn a tenement room into a factory if a market existed for a product produced that way. It often did. Manufacturers often chose to locate in cities because that was where they could find surplus labor. The spread of factories created jobs and jobs meant that more workers were needed to fill those jobs. People to fill those jobs came not just as a result of immigration, but also as a result of internal migration or technological innovations that made getting to those jobs easier. Some of those technological innovations were improvements in the urban infrastructure.

The Brooklyn Bridge connects the boroughs of Manhattan and Brooklyn in New York City. When it opened in May 1883, it was the longest suspension bridge in the world. More importantly, since Brooklyn was not

The Brooklyn Bridge was one of the great engineering marvels of the age. The dumbbell tenements of New York City which sprang up about the same time were not. *(Courtesy of the Library of Congress)*

then part of New York City, the bridge connected the first and third largest cities in the United States at that time. At the opening ceremonies, Abram Hewitt, the iron maker and future mayor of New York City, said, "Every department of human industry is represented, from the quarrying and the cutting of the stones, the mining and smelting of the ores, the conversion of iron into steel by the pneumatic process, to the final shaping of the masses of metal into useful forms, and its reduction into wire, so as to develop in the highest degree the tensile strength which fits it for the work of suspension." Hewitt also discussed the contribution of mechanization to the building of the bridge. "Every tool which the ingenuity of man has invented has somewhere, in some special detail," he said, "contributed its share in the accomplishment of the final result."[3] The bridge, in other words, could never have been built before the era of industrialization.

The way in which labor used those tools also reflected the principles of industrialization, especially the division of labor necessary to build such a huge structure in the most efficient manner possible. One reporter described the digging of the caisson in the sand on the New York side in order to form a base for the tower there as "dozens of workmen hurrying hither and thither with wheelbarrows and hods and spikes and shovels; engines puffing away, lifting huge blocks of stone with huge derricks from the barge at the side of the dock, drawing lumber from the foot of the pier, driving the piles of the cofferdam, and condensing and compressing the air to be used by the submarine workmen" who built the caissons that braced the bridge into the bed of the East River. The reporter also described "men chopping and planing and sawing the immense timbers used in constructing the enormous derricks; others shoveling gravel and sifting sand for the cement; little knots of three driving immense piles through the heavy timbers of the caisson with their sledges and kept steadily at work by an overseer who evidently enjoys his employment."[4] Skilled workers, unskilled immigrants, highly trained engineers: the workers on the Brooklyn Bridge ran the gamut from one end of the American working class to the other.

However, the lasting significance of the Brooklyn Bridge came not from how it was built, but from its effects upon the two cities it connected. As noted in an editorial in the *Railroad Gazette*, published just a week after the bridge opened, "Brooklyn would truly be made part of New York, and the bridge would be of enormous advantage to it. Its [meaning Brooklyn's] beautiful sites for dwellings, now accessible only by a wearisome journey of an hour and a half, would be brought to within 3/4 of an hour of Union Square." As a result, "a very large part of the objections to living in Brooklyn, which have caused rents to half as great as in equally handsome parts, would be obviated."[5] In other words, the bridge opened Brooklyn to commuters. This not only helped Brooklyn grow, but opened up Manhattan real estate to uses other than residential structures for the middle class. When New York City absorbed Brooklyn in 1898, it simply ratified an economic relationship that had developed quickly after the bridge opened.

Noise, overcrowding, public health issues—cities were dirty, often unpleasant places before industrialization began. These problems escalated during this era and new ones developed too, like how to install electrical infrastructure. Overhead wires for telegraphs, telephones, streetcars, and electricity often competed for space along city streets during this period. Large cities also bred new forms of political corruption. Of course, the poor experienced these effects more than the rich, yet the poor continued to stream into America's cities because that is where most of the work was located. The effects of industrialization on cities created problems that reformers tried to solve. The way people lived changed forever as a result.

The Columbian Exhibition and the Real Chicago

The World's Columbian Exposition began in Chicago one year after the 500th anniversary of Christopher Columbus's first landing in North America, the event it commemorated. Like other world's fairs during the late nineteenth and twentieth centuries, the exposition was a celebration of culture, technology, and industry from around the world. Innovations introduced at the fair included the original Ferris Wheel and Juicy Fruit Gum, and even though it had been developed about a decade before, this is where most Americans encountered electric light for the first time. Many fairgoers thought they were visiting a dream. Here were the products of industrialization, placed in an idealized environment built especially for them. Under these conditions, it was easy to forget that this kind of economic transformation had any ill effects at all.

Many of the items on display at the fair were manufactured products. The Manufactures and Liberal Arts Building was the largest roofed building in the world at the time it was built. The structure covered forty acres; the items exhibited in it were divided into thirty-five groups, each group was divided into ten or more classes, and each class was divided into smaller departments. It held everything from firearms to children's dolls; stationery to stoves. The Machinery Hall at the fair illustrated the epitome of mechanization worldwide, but as one guidebook explained, America did it best: "Machinery is doing everything, and more than the hands of man were employed in doing a century ago. Some of the ingenious contrivances one would imagine almost think, so thoroughly do they perform the task assigned them. Here the machinery used in every branch of manufacture is in operation."[6] Although the fair's building could not accommodate entire factories, all the different kinds of machinery displayed together made it easy to see the similarities between technologies that could do similar things.

While the tools of industrialization were on display in these buildings, the way the buildings themselves were organized suggested new ways to cope with the changes that industrialization brought. The Manufactures and Liberal Arts building and the Machinery Hall were part of the

White City, overseen by the Chicago architect Daniel Burnham. The White City earned its name because the buildings were all neoclassical, largely uniform, and, of course, almost entirely white. Observers frequently remarked upon the unity, harmony, and proportion at the Court of Honor, the buildings at the center of the White City. When people saw this gigantic, beautiful planned community, they began to imagine taking some of the qualities of the exposition back to their home communities. Burnham, working alongside the landscape architect Frederick Law Olmsted, made people think of cities as potential works of art, hiding ugly factories through clever zoning.

The Columbian Exposition also pointed the way to alleviate the municipal stresses that industrialization created. "We are tired of polluted air and water, dirty streets, grimy buildings and disordered cities," one planner later explained. "From the 'White City' to . . . [the St. Louis Fair in 1903] the lesson has been impressed that ugliness and inconvenience for the present and the future, will yield to the magic power of the comprehensive plan."[7] Within a few years (delayed as any expensive changes were by the Panic of 1893), the White City helped give rise to the City Beautiful movement, which brought innovations in planning developed at the exposition and elsewhere to cities around the country. Perhaps the most important lesson of the fair was that civic leaders and professional city planners could work together to solve the problems that came with urban life. In the following decades, cities such as Washington, DC, and Philadelphia began to implement master plans designed to improve both the aesthetics of those cities and the living conditions of their inhabitants.

One of the visitors to the Columbian Exposition, the English journalist William Stead, wrote instead about the problems that these planning principles could not solve. His book—*If Christ Came to Chicago!*—pointed out the darker side of urban life near the home of the White City. Tramps were "everywhere in evidence," he wrote when he first visited Chicago in December 1892. "The approach of winter drove [them] from the fields to seek shelter in the towns, which were all overburdened with their own unemployed. Like the frogs in the Egyptian plague, you could not escape from the tramps, go where you would. In the city they wandered through the streets, seeking work and finding none."[8] Surplus labor was the natural outgrowth of the industrial labor policies of major corporations, which preferred having a reserve army of the unemployed to take the place of any workers who demanded too much of their employers.

Urban planning could not solve most of the problems that Stead described. Indeed, such problems grew worse before they got better as the wonders of the fair were experienced in tandem with the economic panic of 1893. "It was marked by unprecedented extremes of poverty, unemployment and unrest," the journalist Ray Stannard Baker later remembered of the economic trouble at time. "I was fascinated by what I was seeing and hearing. What a spectacle! What a human downfall after the magnificence and prodigality of the World's Fair . . . !"[9] At least the victims of this downturn could turn to the churches for help. The Social Gospel, an urban reform movement that played upon the liberal impulse of Christian charity, could help a few people, but government helped none of the suffering since the welfare state did not yet exist. As a result of these periodic downturns in the economy, the working class often went without the basic necessities of life, especially in housing, as the middle class began to move away from large centralized cities like Chicago.

Streetcar Suburbs

Preindustrial urban areas were known as walking cities because the primary means of transportation for everyone was by foot. Inhabitants had to live a short distance from the place of their employment; otherwise they never would have been able to work there. Factories were usually absent from these places because space was at a premium. The suburb emerged as the preferred residence of the urban middle class after 1870. As early as 1873, Chicago boasted nearly 100 streetcar suburbs, strung out like beads along the rail tracks, with a combined population of over 50,000 people. The further development of streetcars and the electric trolleys there and in other cities made the suburbs accessible to more and more people. "On one point the American is determined," observed a writer for the *Atlantic Monthly* in 1902; "he will not live near his work. You shall see him in the morning, one of sixty people in a car built for twenty-four, reading his paper, clinging to a strap, trodden, jostled, smirched . . . after thirty minutes . . . with the roar of the streets in his ears . . . he arrives in his office."[10] When this kind of migration became possible, it relieved the pressure on inner cities to hold people, so that more industrialization could occur in large urban areas. As factories became mechanized, they no longer needed to draw upon large labor supplies, but often employers preferred a large workforce so that competition between potential employees would keep wages down.

Before there were streetcars, there were horsecars; there were also cable cars. The first cable cars were developed in 1867, but did not go into regular use until they debuted in San Francisco in 1873. The leader of the effort there, Andrew Smith Halladie, created them in order to relieve horses of the pain of having to tow cars up the city's many hills. The cable cars were powered by a huge steam engine that moved a cable under various streets. The operator of the cable car would make the car grip the cable in order to move and release it in order to stop. These kinds of cars quickly spread to other cities, but were overtaken in most places by electric streetcars and, later, buses.

The first electric streetcars appeared during the 1880s. Attached to overhead wires, these vehicles used motors that transmitted power from the wires to the wheels. Early streetcars moved at the daunting speed of twelve miles an hour, which was twice as fast as horses could go. (They also did not leave the manure that horses did.) That was enough to at least double the distance that people could commute from work to home and back, thereby making it possible to spread out urban settlement further than ever before. After the turn of the century, streetcars had to compete with automobiles in the streets of major cities. This technology allowed people to spread out even further.

As people began to move out to the end of streetcar lines, the population density decreased, the size of houses increased, and the community structures at both ends of the streetcar line became increasingly distinct. Some people saw the streetcar as a panacea for urban problems as they would allow the poor to escape the slums. In truth, the poor could not afford faster transport every day and had to stay near their place of work at the center of cities. Therefore, the living conditions at the center of cities worsened as skilled workers and middle-class families of even modest means moved out. All that was needed was enough money to afford to take the streetcar to work each day. Even if people could not afford to move, the electric streetcar offered the opportunity to leave the neighborhood at least once in a while. Streetcar firms often built amusement parks at the ends of lines in order to generate business. Coney Island, on the south shore of Brooklyn in New York City, only became a major resort once a local streetcar line first reached there.

An ad from the Chicago area builder Samuel Gross encapsulates the entire process of suburbanization well. The ad shows a series of pictures beginning with an empty lot captioned "Virgin Soil." The next picture depicts a horse-drawn carriage prospecting the site for a new home de-

This graphic from Chicago homebuilder S.E. Gross illustrates just how quickly suburbs could be built on the outskirts of America's booming industrial cities. *(Courtesy of the Library of Congress)*

velopment during winter; the next picture shows the placing of the corner stakes; the next one is captioned "Putting In the Water Pipes and Planting Trees," followed by "Summer Home Building" and the home finished in autumn. A year later, a bustling town stands where once there was nothing. This kind of rapid development would have been completely impossible without the inexpensive production of lumber that industrialization made possible and technical innovations like the balloon frame house—an inexpensive but sturdy style of building pioneered in Chicago, where it made re-creating the city after the Great Fire of 1871 cheaper and more efficient. This was a victory of technology (which made it possible to build quickly) and a sign of the wealth that industrialization created.

Streetcars also did much to spur the growth of central business districts. Because the streetcar lines were arranged like spokes on a wheel, everyone using them had to go into what would come to be known as the downtown areas of major cities in order to disembark or at least to change cars. Large departments stores were just one of many businesses that tended to congregate in these areas so the maximum number of shoppers could reach them easily. The same is true for other industries, especially the white-collar industries that tended to locate in the new tall buildings that sprang up in this same general area. Cities could grow by building up as well as by building out.

Structural Steel and the Elevator

As changes in transportation technology made it possible for people to live further and further away from where they worked, changes in building technology made it possible for more people to work and live in a smaller area. The most important development in building technology during this era was the increase in demand for structural steel. Structural steel was a particular kind of steel that was well-suited for supporting a great deal of weight. Manufacturers began to create large structural shapes that could be used on projects that literally changed the landscape, such as skyscrapers and bridges. American firms quickly mastered this technology well enough to be a primary exporter of these structural shapes around the world.

A key market for structural shapes was for making bridges. Bridges constructed out of iron shapes were common during the mid-nineteenth century, and by the 1880s architects began to use the same technology to build tall buildings. One New York architect actually called his steel frame structure "an iron bridge truss stood on end."[11] Before the invention of structural steel, it was difficult (if not impossible) to make a building higher than about six stories. Anything higher would have required walls so thick on the bottom to support additional weight on top that any windows placed there would have threatened the integrity of the structure. Strong structural steel frames made taller buildings possible. Height was a response to increased land values in central cities, which came about as a result of pressure from increased population. That increased population came from the need to fill jobs as manufacturing concentrated in large cities like Chicago.

The technology to produce steel strong enough for skyscrapers existed as early as the 1860s, but it was at first used exclusively for steel rails. No architect dared to support a building's weight entirely on the iron frame that surrounded it for fear that it would fail and create a calamity. As a result, builders were slow to pick up on the advantages that structural steel offered. Tragedy in this case served as a spur to invention. When downtown Chicago burned up, investors saw an unprecedented opportunity to build up an urban area quickly and efficiently. The desire of both builders and occupants to make money quickly led Chicago architects, especially Louis Sullivan, to experiment with this new building design during the 1880s for the first time. The last building built of masonry in Chicago went up in 1891. Although it reached a height of sixteen stories, its walls had to be six feet thick at the base, which limited the room for office space. In the age of industrialization, leaving money on the table in this manner was simply unacceptable.

By the turn of the twentieth century, skyscrapers had become the norm in the downtown areas of large cities nationwide. They were erected using modern construction processes that depended upon the division of labor and mechanization. The improvements in strength that steel frame construction provided also made it possible to increase the window space of such buildings. This changed the look of tall buildings from both inside and out, making them less classical and more modern. Architects could also decorate the lower stories of these new buildings more elaborately, changing the way that cities looked to passersby at street level too. As a result, the urban environment became increasingly separated from nature. Now even people who were not cooped up in office buildings could spend their whole days without seeing ground, except in the many city parks developed in this era that served as reminders of the pastoral lives that so many urban dwellers had left behind.

Obviously, bigger buildings meant more people in them. This meant more commerce packed into a smaller area. As one observer in New York City noted in 1897, "The skyscraper . . . gathers into a single edifice an extraordinary number of activities, which otherwise would be widely separated. Each building is an almost complete city, often comprising within its walls banks and insurance offices, post office and telegraph office, business exchanges, restaurants, clubrooms and shops." Skyscrapers, the observer continued, also served as retail palaces: "The business man can provide himself with clothes, shoes, cigars, stationery and baths; receive and dispatch his mail and his telegrams; speculate; consult his lawyer . . . ; and transact his own business, all without leaving the building in which his office is located."[12] Business owners who had to conduct business with clients outside the building could use the telephone (another invention of this era) rather than ever leave the office. Many of the large monopolies that developed during the 1890s were conceived and executed in such buildings, where white-collar industries of all kinds tended to congregate.

Since nobody wanted to walk up thirty stories on a regular basis, the invention of the elevator was also a prerequisite for the development of skyscrapers. The first reliable elevator was invented in 1857 by Elisha Graves Otis for a five-story building. Improvements in speed, power, and safety were required before electric elevators could carry people to the top of tall buildings in an efficient manner. This changed the way that real estate was valued in such structures. Previous to the elevator, high floors were cheaper because of the stairs. With elevators, higher floors were often favored because of the views they provided.

When such technologies were applied to living quarters, they increased the number of people who could live closer to where they worked. The first apartment building was built in New York City in 1869. At first, these structures were extremely controversial, as wealth usually bought space and separation from one's neighbors. To counter this kind of prejudice, New Yorkers developed the idea of the cooperative (or "co-op"), which gave residents a financial interest in the building. The income tax, designed to confiscate more of the proceeds of industrialization to redistribute to the body politic, prevented the richest Americans from spending their money on urban mansions. Once New York real estate became simply too expensive for all but the greatest fortunes, expensive apartments grew to be a popular alternative.

Although the urban rich and urban poor both lived in apartment houses, the poor had much less room in their apartments. New York's famous dumbbell tenements were the model for urban housing in that city and elsewhere. They came about as the result of a design contest conducted by the journal *Plumber and Sanitary Engineer* in 1878. The winner would be the architect who could combine safety and convenience with the maximum profitability for the investor. The fact that the buildings had to be able to fit a 25- by 100-foot lot was a clear sign that the last criterion was ultimately the most important one. Urban real estate had been a good investment for excess capital since the early nineteenth century. Now, slumlords could invest their profits from other industries into apartment buildings, thereby taking advantage of working-class people both on and off the job.

James E. Ware's winning design was called a dumbbell tenement because it was shaped like a dumbbell, five or six stories tall with an indentation on each side of the building to let in light and air. Unfortunately, the amount of light and air getting to most apartments was minimal because these tenements were placed side by side. Four families lived on most floors, which had fourteen rooms total and only two bathrooms. In their heyday, tenements housed three-quarters of New York City's population. These tenements were often factories of a kind. Residents slept in the same place where they rolled cigars or hemmed garments. Problems with this design were recognized immediately. One sanitary engineer called the prize "the most ingenious design for dungeons."[13] The Tenement House Act of 1901 outlawed this design in New York City.

In order to escape the difficult conditions in American cities during the era of industrialization, many urban families moved west. The implementation of the Homestead Act in 1863 gave many urban dwellers a chance at a new life. The law had been blocked by southern states before secession because they feared that northern migrants would ensure that the new states in the West outlaw slavery and perhaps end slavery everywhere in the United States. Now, poor urbanites could stake a claim to a plot of 160 acres simply by farming on it for five years. Congress thought the Homestead Act a solution to urban overcrowding and the need to develop the West. Free land drew people to the natural resources of the West, but it was industrialization in the East that created the market that made those resources valuable.

Notes

1. Thomas Bender, "Urbanization," in *The Reader's Companion to American History*, ed. Eric Foner and John A. Garaty (Boston: Houghton Mifflin, 1991), 1102.

2. Samuel P. Hayes, *The Response to Industrialism, 1885–1914*, 2nd ed. (Chicago: University of Chicago Press, 1995), 47.

3. "Opening Ceremonies of the New York and Brooklyn Bridge," May 24, 1883 (Brooklyn, NY: 1883), 49.

4. In David McCullough, *The Great Bridge: The Epic Story of the Building of the Brooklyn Bridge* (New York: Simon & Schuster, 1972), 272.

5. In Alan Trachtenberg, *Brooklyn Bridge: Fact and Symbol*, 2nd ed. (Chicago: University of Chicago Press, 1979), 111.

6. The Religious Herald, *Picturesque Chicago and Guide to the World's Fair* (Hartford: D.S. Moseley, 1893), 210.

7. In William Henry Wilson, *The City Beautiful Movement* (Baltimore: Johns Hopkins University Press, 1989), 71.

8. William T. Stead, *If Christ Came to Chicago!* (Chicago: Laird & Lee, 1894), 17.

9. In Nell Irvin Painter, *Standing at Armageddon: The United States, 1877–1919* (New York: W.W. Norton, 1987), 117.

10. Charles M. Skinner, "The American Will Not Live Near His Work," in *Visions of Technology*, ed. Richard Rhodes (New York: Simon & Schuster, 1999), 39.

11. In Jim Rasenberger, *High Steel: The Daring Men Who Built the World's Greatest Skyline, 1881 to the Present* (New York: Harper Collins, 2004), 40.

12. In Ric Burns and James Sanders, *New York: An Illustrated History* (New York: Alfred A. Knopf, 1999), 233–235.

13. In Roy Lubove, *The Progressives and the Slums: Tenement House Reform in New York City, 1890–1917* (Pittsburgh: University of Pittsburgh Press, 1962), 32.

The West

Q. *What was the significance of the frontier in American history?*

In 1893 the American Historical Association held its annual convention in Chicago so that attendees could see the World's Columbian Exposition there. One of the attendees was a professor from the nearby University of Wisconsin in Madison, Frederick Jackson Turner. The speech he gave has proven to be the most significant paper in the history of the American historical profession. "The Significance of the Frontier in American History" was Turner's first stab at what has come to be known as the Frontier Thesis. This argument suggests that the continuing migration of Americans toward the westward edges of the continent had made America more democratic and Americans upwardly mobile. In his speech Turner also noted a recent report from the government's Census Bureau that the frontier had recently been completely filled up with people.

While the original version of Turner's speech did not say anything about industrialization, over the course of his long career, Turner continually adapted his Frontier Thesis to fit the changing circumstances that industrialization created. By 1910 he observed, "The transformations through which the United States is passing in our own day are so profound, so far-reaching, that it is hardly an exaggeration to say that we are witnessing the birth of a new nation in America." Industrialization was a major cause of these dramatic changes, especially with respect to the "revolution in the social and economic structure of this country during the past two decades." Turner called those changes "comparable to what occurred when independence was declared and the constitution was formed, or to the changes wrought by the era which began half a century ago, the era of Civil War and Reconstruction."[1] Since those changes involved the concentration of the wealth from industrialization into fewer and fewer hands, Turner was afraid that the power that wealth brought might destroy the democratic ideals that he valued so highly.

Westward the Course of Empire Takes Its Way is the subtitle of this famous print. To most Americans, railroads symbolized the coming of civilization to a west that Native Americans occupied, but were not exploiting to its full potential. *(Courtesy of the Library of Congress)*

The men who created that wealth thought otherwise. As Turner explained, they "regard themselves as pioneers under changed conditions, carrying on the old work of developing the natural resources of the nation, compelled by the constructive fever in their veins . . . to seek new avenues of action and of power, to chop new clearings, to find new trails, to expand the horizon of the nation's activity, and to extend the scope of their dominion."[2] But Turner, not entirely convinced that the industrialists were right, saw a threat to democracy in the concentration of economic power in so few hands, even if that power could invoke precedent in order to justify its position. To Turner, this accumulation of wealth accompanied the passing of the significance of the frontier, but in fact industrial power was essential to developing the West long before all the cheap land there disappeared.

The key instrument through which industrialization acted upon the West was the railroad. The buffalo, for example, were once a potent symbol of the American West's limitless abundance. As people from the East moved west, sportsmen—including tourists—shot guns made by machines out of trains made in factories at herds of buffalo. These animals had fed and clothed Native Americans for centuries. Approximately

1 million buffalo a year were killed during the peak of the slaughter. So many died that when future president Theodore Roosevelt arrived in the Dakotas in 1883, he had terrible trouble finding one to kill so that he could stuff and mount its head. While some carcasses got turned into trophies, blankets, or hats, countless others were left to rot in the sun. Still others, in these days before rubber production, were used to make leather belts that drove the machines that made industrialization possible. The slaughter of the buffalo was one of many changes that Americans brought to the West through the products of industrialization for the benefit of further industrialization.

As the West itself industrialized, it filled up with people from the East. That is when the citizens of the West became a major market for the finished goods that industrialization produced. Mail-order retailers like Sears and Montgomery Ward sold all types of goods to people all over the country. Both retailers were based in Chicago since their growth was dependent upon the development of western markets and the railroad systems that all converged upon that city. When California entered the country in 1850, it was so far removed from the rest of the country that it was like a distant island. Then, thanks to a series of transcontinental railroads, its agricultural bounty could be consumed in eastern cities even before the turn of the twentieth century. As technology and transportation improved, all kinds of goods from the West developed worldwide markets. However, no other Western products were as famous as the region's cows.

Refrigerated Transport

Cows were an important resource in America during the nineteenth century because meat was a much more valuable commodity then than it is today. It was a luxury that industrialization turned into a regular meal for most Americans. However, turning cows into steaks—that is, raising, transporting, tending, killing, and preserving the animals—took a lot of capital, a lot of work, and huge investments in new technologies by large meatpacking companies. It was only after the materialization of extensive infrastructure required for a nationwide beef industry that cows that had been fattened on the open grasslands of the West could become widely available in the East. People made fortunes feeding cattle in one region and selling them in another. The same would be true for other perishable foods.

The first market for western beef in the East was developed by packers who transported live cows eastward. They had to deal with an enormous amount of waste since at that time a market existed for only a limited portion of the cow. They also had to deal with the deaths of many animals along the way; not to mention the fact that the cows became significantly thinner in transit since it was impossible for them to graze during their journey. The production of dressed beef (beef that had already been slaughtered and prepared for purchase) began in Chicago during the 1860s. The transportation of dressed meat instead of live cows carried less risk and was more efficient. However, it also required the development of ice-cooled, refrigerated railway cars; otherwise the meat would have gone bad before it arrived in the East.

Despite experiments in the early days of American railroads, the real growth in the use of meatpacking technology came after the Civil War. That is when packers first tried to ship dressed meat across the country, preserving it with ice cut from lakes and streams along the way. Whenever the ice melted, the car stopped at a new station to get more. This sounds like a lot of trouble (and it was), but ice would continue to be the only way to chill perishable food on railway cars until the 1950s. The most successful and best-remembered of many efforts to perfect the refrigerated railcar came from the packer Gustavus Swift. Despite high expenses, Swift made selling dressed meat profitable, still underselling eastern slaughterhouses and still profiting with each sale. Swift grew to become one of five large meatpackers whose factories were concentrated in the Midwest, especially around Chicago.

Thanks to new chemical research laboratories, the Big Five meatpackers could turn a pig or a steer into much more than just meat. According to one observer who visited the Chicago stockyards during the Columbian Exposition, "Everything—without particularizing too closely—every single thing that appertains to a slaughtered beef is sold and put to use." The list of uses was quite daunting:

> The horns become the horn of commerce; the straight lengths of leg bone go to the cutlery-makers and others; the entrails become sausage casings; their contents make fertilizing material; the livers, hearts, tongues and tails, and the stomachs, that become tripe, all are sold over the butchers' counters of the nation; the knuckle-bones are ground up into bone-meal for various uses; the blood is dried and sold as a powder for commercial purposes; the bladders are dried and sold to druggists, tobacconists, and others; the fat goes into oleomargarine, and from the hoofs and feet and other parts come glue and oil and fertilizing ingredients.[3]

The beef industry, in other words, was about a lot more than a nice, juicy steak. It provided many of the raw materials of modern life.

The concept behind this kind of product multipurposing is known as economies of scope. These extra products were what made killing and selling animals on such a dramatic scale profitable. They provided the margin between profit and loss. The same kinds of multipurposing also occurred with pigs. That was the source of the famous line about using "everything but the squeal," which was picked up by Upton Sinclair and put in his classic 1906 novel, *The Jungle*. Using every part of an animal cut down on industrial pollution, a serious problem around Chicago earlier in the century when this production process was just beginning to become centralized.

Chicago was the border city between east and west. Not only cows, but lumber, wheat, and other commodities made their way through Chicago on their way east as nearly every railroad in the region bisected or terminated in that city. The supply chains and markets for all these commodities demonstrated the relationship between the two regions. One could not develop without the other. Resources traveled east, while people and finished products traveled west. The economic futures of both regions were inexorably linked, especially as the West became where much of America's food was produced.

Eventually other perishable foods began to travel east even if they did not necessarily stop in Chicago. During the 1890s, for example, California became the point of origin for much of the fruit consumed in America. In 1891 the essayist Charles Dudley Warner called California "our Italy." He was not just talking about the potential to vacation there. "From San Bernadino and Redlands, Riverside, Pomona, Ontario and Santa Anita," he wrote, "San Gabriel and all the way to Los Angeles, is almost one continuous fruit garden, the green areas only emphasized by wastes yet unclaimed."[4] Without markets, all this fruit was useless. Therefore, the application of the same iced railway cars used for meat was essential for the fruit industry's growth. While fruit might not spoil if shipped unrefrigerated, this technology made it possible for California fruit to enter eastern markets at reasonable prices by keeping more of the fruit fresh than would be possible without ice at all. Without refrigeration, California agriculture, like much of the rest of American agriculture, would have been dependent upon less perishable crops like wheat.

Factories in the Fields

Small farmers and their families, of course, had to do all the different kinds of work on a farm themselves. They had no labor to divide because they had no money to hire help. The naturalist John Muir, who grew up on a Wisconsin wheat farm, remembered that "long before the great labor-saving machines came to our help" his early days "abounded in trying work—cradling in the long, sweaty dog-days, raking and binding, stacking, thrashing—it often seemed to me that our fierce, over-industrious way of getting the grain from the ground was too closely connected with grave-digging."[5] Working from dawn to dusk, the family's very life dependent upon its success, farming families often found their work unrewarding in both the financial and metaphorical senses.

Eventually technology made it possible to extract more from the land than ever before. The industrialization of agriculture in the United States was a gradual process. Some crops, like wheat, have been harvested by mechanical devices since the mid-nineteenth century. Yet harvesting is just one step in a long process of bringing that crop from the field to the market. Other crops, like apples, grow on trees in irregular shapes and in irregular positions. The human eye is an absolute necessity to allow farmworkers to pick such a fruit and handle it carefully enough so that it will not be bruised. Therefore, apple picking could not be mechanized. Because of the growing size of California wheat farms and because there has always been a shortage of labor in American agriculture, large farmers, particularly wheat farmers, mechanized early. Experiments with steam tractors began in 1871 and continued through the 1880s. They cut the size of a typical threshing crew from twenty-one or twenty-two workers to as little as two. The machines were expensive, costing between $3,000 and $5,000 each. However, some farmers calculated that they could afford to buy one simply by selling all their animals. While these machines ultimately proved to be faster and more efficient than men or even horses, wheat harvesting was just one part of the process of raising just one crop. The introduction of the division of labor to California agriculture proved much more important than mechanization in the long run because it affected every part of the process for harvesting every crop, including crops for which production was difficult to mechanize. By 1900 steam combines were used to harvest about two-thirds of the wheat in the state.

The successful use of technology for some crops at some steps in the production process encouraged the mechanization of all kinds of farm work. "No farmer can expect to make the farm pay by hand work, as it was done a number of years ago, when the scythe, the sickle, the grain cradle, the hand rake, the flail and the hay fork were in use," wrote William Crozier in his 1884 treatise, *How the Farm Pays*. "He is forced now to use the mower, and the reaper which now binds the sheaves and leaves them ready for the shock; the horse rake, the threshing machine and the hay and grain elevators."[6] The bigger the farm was, the better it could take advantage of this kind of industrialization. As was the case with the original factories, the first movers gained the greatest advantage from these industrial changes.

Such innovations were inevitably very expensive. Since all the new farm machinery available during this era was protected by patents, starting a modern farm cost a new farmer what would have been a fortune to any of the older generation of farmers. As a result, many small western farmers took on debt in order to compete and were eventually forced out of business. "The entire agricultural regions of our country," argued critic William Moody, "are crowded with loan agents, representing capital from all the great money centers of the world, who are making loans and taking mortgages upon the farms to an amount that, in the aggregate, appears to be beyond calculation."[7] To save money, these factories in the fields often relied upon itinerant labor to run their machines, creating the same kind of class tensions that characterized a steel mill or a slaughterhouse.

Thanks to access to machines and the capital to buy them, the average size of a western farm skyrocketed. The bonanza wheat farms in the high plains of the Dakotas and Minnesota could grow to the size of over 10,000 acres. The clear, flat land was perfect for the use of steam tractors. These kinds of enterprises were magnets for European investment, which imported the product of such farms into their continent to feed the starving masses there. It was not just the fact that machinery could do the work that mattered. The way that the machinery was powered meant that the work could be done faster. In fact, the benefits of this new source of power were manifold. "For as horse power is much cheaper than human power, so steam is cheaper than horses," explained Crozier, "and it has the advantage that when it is not at work it has not to be fed, nor is an engine subject to disease which shortens the useful life of a horse so much."[8] The advantages of mechanization were so great all around that those farmers who did not invest and grow their holdings in order to pay for those holdings risked being undersold and put out of business by those who did since the efficiencies of industrialized agriculture were staggering. People around the world benefited from the product of industrialized agriculture, as technology proved Thomas Malthus's gloomy early nineteenth-century prediction of mass starvation wrong.

There were significant hazards to large-scale farming; bad weather, insect infestation, even a bountiful harvest could make it difficult to pay back loans if the market price for whatever crop a farmer produced went down as a result of successful farming everywhere. The losers in this process often became tenant farmers, forced to rent other people's land. Itinerant farmers faced an even more troubling situation, needing to wander from place to place in order to find any kind of agricultural employment. Just as in the urban factories, the rich got richer and the rural poor got poorer during the age of industrialization. In fact, many other failed farmers and especially their children ended up in cities, because that was where the jobs were. Native Americans, stuck on reservations, had nowhere else to go.

The Dawes Severalty Act and Native American Education

Perhaps the primary historical flaw of Frederick Jackson Turner's Frontier Thesis is that it does not sufficiently acknowledge the significance of the Native Americans who occupied America before Europeans ever settled the continent. By the time the era of industrialization arrived, those Native Americans who remained in the West had been completely overwhelmed by the superior military forces and vast numbers of European Americans who had arrived in the region over the previous decades. The Indian wars of the late nineteenth century were mostly to force Native Americans onto reservations, a policy that began during the 1840s. Americans justified such actions by arguing that Native Americans were not using the good lands, so it made sense to force them onto the bad lands. As the *New York Herald*, a newspaper with a national circulation, argued when miners eyed the Black Hills during the early 1870s, "It is inconsistent with our civilization and with common sense to allow the Indian to roam over a country as fine as that around the Black Hills, preventing its development in order that he may shoot game and scalp his neighbors."[9] Once enough settlers arrived, they pushed Native Americans off the marginal land too.

When confined to reservations, Native Americans had to adapt to an entirely new economic system and lifestyle in order to survive. Surprisingly, early reformers, in their attitude toward the value of Native American societies, resembled the people who wanted to push the Indians off their land. Many reformers felt that it was cruel and unusual punishment to allow Native Americans to live the way that they always had. "We have encroached upon their means of subsistence without furnishing them any proper return," noted Julius Seelye of Amherst College in 1880; "we have not hesitated to drive them off [their land] for our profit, without regard to theirs."[10] While undoubtedly well-meaning, the assumption here was that Native Americans were incapable of helping themselves. White industrial superiority was seen as proof of racial superiority.

The wholesale slaughter of the buffalo essentially forced most Native Americans on the Great Plains onto government-sponsored reservations. Buffalo were not only a food source for the tribes located there; they provided clothing, shelter, saddles, rope, and many other articles essential to their lifestyles. The transition was not easy. "During the winter of 1886–'87, destitution and actual starvation prevailed to an alarming extent among certain tribes of Indians in the Northwest Territory who once lived bountifully on the buffalo," wrote William T. Hornaday in *The Extermination of the American Bison* in 1889. "Heart-rending stories of suffering and cannibalism continue to come in from what was once the buffalo plains."[11] Trains brought not only buffalo hunters to the West, but also people who fenced in land and prevented the tribes from living off it as hunters or gatherers. In other words, the onset of industrial civilization destroyed the Native American way of life. The American government gave the tribes no alternative but to assimilate.

Indian reformers wanted to ease the Native Americans down the path of integration into the larger society, which meant teaching them to be consumers. "Discontent with the tepee and the starving rations of the Indian camp in winter is needed to get the Indians out of the blanket and into trousers," wrote a representative of Friends of the Indian in 1896. The trousers he meant were "trousers with a pocket in them, and a pocket that aches to be filled with dollars!"[12] Native Americans who farmed on reservations produced crops for sale on the open market, crops that would bring in money for consumption of goods manufactured in the East, the kind of consumption that white capitalists approved. Any way of acquiring dollars, through agriculture or wage labor, meant that Native Americans would spend those dollars, thereby helping producers sell the surplus that industrialization created. Those who did not fend for themselves were at the mercy of corrupt bureaucrats who ran the reservations and concessionaires who contracted with the government to provide inferior goods to a group that had no voice in Washington to protest such treatment.

The stated purpose of the Dawes Severalty Act, sponsored by Senator Henry Dawes of Massachusetts and passed in 1887, was to give Native Americans the same commercial opportunities white people had in order to integrate them into the American economic system. Under the act,

Native American children who attended boarding schools like this one in Carlisle, Pennsylvania, learned not only about mainstream culture, they also learned trade skills like metalworking so that they could participate successfully in the free enterprise system. *(Courtesy of the Library of Congress)*

land owned by Native American tribes was broken up and assigned to individual families to work on their own. While this was supposed to promote Indian entrepreneurship, many of these allotments were eventually rented to whites. Even before the Severalty Act passed, reformers emphasized the potential commercial benefits of harnessing the capitalist impulses of Native American children. In her best-selling 1881 reform tract *A Century of Dishonor*, novelist Helen Hunt Jackson cited the productivity of the Cheyenne and Arapahoe, despite their hardships, as evidence of their capitalist potential: "The school children have, by their earnings, bought one hundred head of cattle; 451,000 pounds of freight have been transported by the Indians during the year; they have also worked at making brick, chopping wood, making hay, hauling wood, and splitting and hauling rails; and have earned thereby $712[.]25."[13] That was a lot of money for Native Americans.

After the passage of the Dawes Act, reformers turned to education and successfully got the government to sponsor Native American schools.

Unfortunately for the families involved, the federal schools that the government established were boarding schools far away from reservations out west. They were designed to get students to reject key aspects of their centuries-old cultures in the name of self-reliance in the modern world. Displaced from the environment where they grew up, many Native American children died of disease or mistreatment far away from home. Perhaps acceptance of industrial values was better for Native Americans than starvation, but the transition process was particularly wrenching for people who had to come so far, so fast. The destruction of the environment in the original homelands of so many tribes affected them first, but this kind of damage eventually adversely affected Americans of all kinds.

Notes

1. Frederick Jackson Turner, *The Frontier in American History* (New York: Henry Holt, 1920), 311.

2. Turner, 319.

3. In William Cronon, *Nature's Metropolis: Chicago and the Great West* (New York: W.W. Norton, 1991), 250.

4. In Douglas Cazaux Sackman, *Orange Empire: California and the Fruits of Eden* (Berkeley: University of California Press, 2005), 30.

5. John Muir, "The Story of My Boyhood and Youth," in *Muir: Nature Writings* (New York: Library of America, 1997), 107.

6. William Crozier and Peter Henderson, *How the Farm Pays* (New York: Peter Henderson & Co., 1884), 275.

7. William Moody, *Land and Labor in the United States* (New York: Charles Scribner's Sons, 1883), 86.

8. Crozier and Henderson, 299.

9. In Richard Slotkin, *The Fatal Environment: The Myth of the Frontier in the Age of Industrialization, 1800–1890* (New York: Harper & Row, 1986), 450.

10. In Helen Hunt Jackson, *A Century of Dishonor* (New York: Harper & Brothers, 1881), 1–2.

11. William T. Hornaday, *The Extermination of the American Bison*, in *Report of the United States National Museum* (Washington, DC: Government Printing Office, 1889), 2:527.

12. In Jackson Lears, *Rebirth of a Nation* (New York: HarperCollins, 2009), 202.

13. Jackson, 101.

6 Environment

*Q. What were the environmental costs of
industrialization to the public at large?*

During the late 1860s, there were about 1,000 butchers in New Orleans, Louisiana. They dumped the refuse created by the slaughter of 300,000 animals a year into the Mississippi River, one and a half miles upstream from where the city got its water supply.[1] Many slaughterhouses were located near the municipal waterworks. The remnants of slaughtered animals not dumped into the river were often dumped and left to rot in the butchers' backyards. As a result of this situation, cholera and yellow fever had been rampant in the city for decades, except when the Union Army had occupied New Orleans during the Civil War. A state legislator who proposed a bill that would have required slaughterhouses to move upriver called their location at the time "a pesthole[,] poisoning air and water."[1] There were also widespread complaints that the existing slaughterhouses were so filthy that the meat they produced was not fit to eat.

There had been many attempts to regulate slaughterhouses in New Orleans before the war, but the strong butchers' lobby had beaten them back. What changed this situation was the new Republican government that controlled the state after the fall of the Confederacy. When Union troops left, sanitation reverted to a low priority. In order to rectify this situation, the New Orleans City Council passed a weak ordinance to regulate slaughterhouses in 1866. In 1869 a new state legislature with a Republican majority for the first time passed a stronger law. Its intention was to grant a monopoly to a new, single slaughterhouse where displaced butchers could all practice their trade. It was to be located south of the city, thereby sparing the people of New Orleans animal parts and other slaughterhouse waste in their drinking water. The city leaders hoped that a new, modern slaughterhouse might also attract more of the Texas cattle trade to their port, instead of its travel to the population centers on the East Coast entirely by rail.

In 1873 the United States Supreme Court let the law stand in what has come to be known as the *Slaughterhouse Cases* (although a new state legislature would break up the monopoly just over ten years later). The historical importance of the dispute comes from the dissenting opinion of Justice Stephen Field, who argued that a government-run slaughterhouse was the beginning of government intervention into just about everything. If a monopoly "may be granted for structures in which animal food is prepared for market," he wrote, "they may be equally granted for structures in which [other] food is prepared. They may be granted for any of the pursuits of human industry, even in its most simple and common forms. Indeed, upon the theory on which the exclusive privileges granted by the act in question are sustained, there is no monopoly, in the most odious form, which may not be upheld."[3] In short, Field argued that the rights of a few business owners were more important than the rights of the citizens of New Orleans to live in a healthy environment.

The majority opinion in the *Slaughterhouse Cases* was the first time that anyone had thought of applying the Fourteenth Amendment of the United States Constitution to individual states. Because this was a milestone in the history of American law, the fact that the circumstances of the case dealt with the urban environment has been largely forgotten. In 1886 the Court in *Santa Clara v. Southern Pacific Railroad* flipped on the question of the rights of corporations, reversing the precedent set by the earlier decision and agreeing on the principle behind Field's dissent. Corporations now had the same rights under the Fourteenth Amendment that people do. The ideas first set out by Field in the *Slaughterhouse Cases* were therefore a landmark in the history of American law because they mark the beginning of a rationale that has made it difficult to regulate corporate power down to this day. When his arguments became law after 1886, they gave all corporations, in effect, the right to freely pollute the environment.

In economic terms, the pollution that butchers dumped into the Mississippi River was what we now call an externality. An externality is a cost not reflected on a company's balance sheet that society ends up paying instead. That means it was an effect of the butchers' normal operation that hurt society at large, yet the perpetrators of that damage were not held accountable to clean it up or even rectify it. Businesses often generate externalities, but those involving the environment were particularly prevalent during the late nineteenth century, when the

American economy was largely based on resource extraction. Once blessed by the Supreme Court, corporate personhood not only allowed large companies to continue to pollute and do other forms of environmental damage, but it prevented the kind of government regulation that might have limited a whole slew of industrialization's negative effects. Eventually, people came to recognize the impact of industrialization upon the environment. Unfortunately, by then it was often too late to reverse the damage.

Oysters

New York City was once famous for the quality and quantity of its oysters. Drawn from the waters surrounding the city, they were sold in beaten-down shacks near the waterfront and at the finest hotels, eaten with gusto by the rich and poor alike. "Oysters pickled, stewed, baked, roasted, fried and scalloped;" wrote one observer in 1859, "oysters made into soups, patties and puddings; oysters with condiments and without condiments; oysters for breakfast, dinner and supper; oysters without stint or limit—fresh as the fresh air, and almost as abundant—are daily offered to the palates of the Manhattanese, and appreciated with all the gratitude which such bounty of nature ought to inspire."[4] There were even oyster cellars, dens of vice and sin that attracted the bottom of society as much as the tavern.

Such a bounty of oysters did not always come naturally. Since oysters sometimes failed to grow to the size that New Yorkers most desired, entrepreneurs brought Chesapeake oysters north and dropped them in places in the harbor that they leased from the state. There, free from the immediate competition of other oysters, the Chesapeake invaders could grow fat and tasty off the nutrients in the open water. Old Dutch families based on Staten Island grew wealthy using this strategy.

With the coming of industrialization, the quality and quantity of oysters began to decline. The first reason for this decline was obvious to everyone: factories brought pollution and pollution ruined oyster beds. Oysters are filter feeders. They pick their food out of the water surrounding them as it runs through their shells so what is in the water gets in the oyster. The first beds to be abandoned because of industrial pollution were north of the city near the mouth of the Harlem River during the 1870s. During the 1890s, people realized that there was a connection between oysters and typhoid. Not just industrial waste, but the waste of humans who

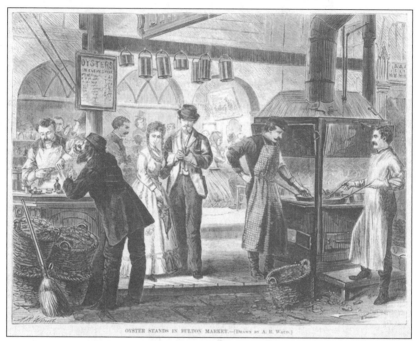

OYSTER STANDS IN FULTON MARKET.—[Drawn by A. R. Waud.]

Now a luxury, oysters were once considered working-class food in New York before pollution destroyed many oyster beds in waterways around the city.

work in all the industries located in and around cities can infect oysters if it gets into the water they filter. The industry turned to seeding new beds in clean water or shipping in oysters from elsewhere to feed what demand remained after the pollution scares.

In 1916 most of the oyster beds in New York Harbor were condemned by the local public health authorities after a typhoid fever outbreak was definitively traced to the refuse from a huge open sewer line in New Jersey. The oystermen who seeded beds in the harbor had to pull up their entire product that they could find. To make matters worse for them, demand disappeared when people realized that eating New York's oysters could make them sick. What local oyster industry remained was based away from the city and the pollution it produced. Nevertheless, since the oyster bedders could not move every oyster that they had planted, oysters remained in New York Harbor as late as 1951. A few old timers still secretly harvested and ate them, despite state law. Sometimes they became horribly ill as a result.

The other effect of industrialization upon oyster beds involved how they were harvested. This industry was once the province of lone fishermen, operating oyster rakes to harvest what they could find around New York. However, such methods could not keep up with the insatiable demand in New York and elsewhere. Steam-powered oyster dredges first appeared during the 1870s. By churning up the mud at the bottom of an oyster bed, they could haul up seven or eight bushels at once. By 1880 steam power had increased the number of oysters in the annual catch to a level twelve times greater than when fishermen simply worked alone. In the same way that Bluefin tuna have been overfished today, taking so many oysters out of the water at once limited their ability to breed. This, in turn, limited the number of oysters available in the future, which decreased supply and therefore drove up prices.

The lesson here applies not just to oysters, but also to many other environmental resources extracted during this era. For most of the nineteenth century, people did not recognize that natural resources had limits, particularly a natural resource that seemed as bountiful as the oysters surrounding New York City. Nevertheless, if too many oysters are harvested, not as many will come back next year. If too many are harvested year after year, they may disappear entirely (at least the ones clean enough to eat). Industrialization, in the form of machines like steam dredges, severely tested the limits of all kinds of natural resources. When the extraction process became mechanized, the natural balance of consumption and production was disturbed. While some kinds of oysters became extinct during this era, there were other reefs to rely upon. Even the oysters in beds that were heavily harvested could come back over the course of a short life cycle. When loggers cut down forests, on the other hand, the impact is essentially permanent.

The Destruction of the Longleaf Pine

Perhaps the clearest sign of civilization arriving in a new area was the clearing of the landscape. Early in the nineteenth century, huge sections of the American Midwest were nothing but forests. Those forests were cleared, often by backbreaking manual labor, so that houses could be built and farming could begin. As time passed, new uses for the timber cut to provide shelter and subsistence emerged. Railroads, for example, required countless cords of wood in order to provide the ties that linked the steel rails together. Other uses depended upon the industrial needs in a particular climate. California was the home of giant redwood trees. These trees resisted rot and insects even when dead. Therefore, they had tremendous value as building material and disappeared quickly, starting in the 1850s. While it sometimes took squadrons of men to cut them down, technological innovations like steam-powered saws led to the cutting down of entire forests of these majestic trees. Today, only a few remain standing. Without the efforts of early environmentalists there would probably be none left.

Such methods contributed to the spread of clear-cutting other trees in other regions later. The Southeast, all the way from Virginia to Florida, was once dominated by longleaf pine forest. These trees were the source of six important products: longleaf pine gum, crude turpentine, spirits of turpentine, tar, pitch, and rosin. Taken together, these products were known as naval stores because they were all used to keep wooden ships from rotting. Tar was also used to grease the wheels on wagons and to preserve fence posts. These uses indicate that this was an old industry, so old as to predate industrialization. The timber products industry, which included both wood and naval stores, was the South's largest manufacturing industry until 1920 (even though naval stores probably should have been classified as an agricultural product, which would have made it second to cotton production).

Most of the first workers in the naval stores industry were slaves. Their job was to tap the sap of a set number of longleaf pines in a given day and to boil down the sap into a usable product. Under the task system, they had only one job to do and free time after that job was done. The task system remained long after slavery disappeared. Poor blacks and convict labor were the chief laborers in this industry after emancipation. The methods they used were mostly the same as before the Civil War. "Boxing" meant using a special ax with an elongated head to cut a hole at the base of the pine tree's trunk. The size of the hole increased as the tree's gum emerged, but the boxes were deliberately cut so as to avoid killing the tree. After the boxing was complete, workers "cornered" the trees in order to make the sap emerge. This involved removing two triangular chips from the tree immediately above the box. At that point, the sap was collected in buckets perhaps three or four times each season. A large tree might be boxed in three or four different places.

While none of this necessarily killed the tree while the process was occurring, the damage to the tree in the long run was considerable. Many pine trees died after being boxed. Even those that continued to live did not grow back to anywhere near the same height. Some that did bear seeds did not always replace themselves thanks to the fondness of feral hogs for their seedlings. The result was the exhaustion of the ecosystem. By 1896 one observer noted that "the forests invaded by turpentine orcharding present, in five or six years after they have been abandoned, a picture of ruin and desolation painful to behold, and in view of the destruction of the seedlings and the younger growth all hope of the reforestation of these magnificent forests is excluded."[5] Many producers followed up tapping by clear-cutting or by controlled burning each year in order to improve accessibility.

During the late nineteenth century, new railroads made clear-cutting longleaf pine forest quickly and efficiently much easier. By 1880 lumber companies had already denuded all the land close to streams and railroads and were starting to destroy the virgin pine forests in less accessible areas. Many of these former forests became marginal farmland. The industry survived the destruction it brought by gradually moving further south, a process that had begun before the Civil War, but accelerated afterward as the industry grew. Of course, this movement only compounded the environmental impact of the naval stores industry by bringing it to new areas. During the late 1940s, this industry became technologically obsolete as new ways were found to make turpentine and its related products. Nevertheless, the environmental damage inflicted by the naval stores industry persisted even as longleaf pine stands were threatened by other factors. By 2000 only 2.2 percent of the original land covered by longleaf pine forest in the United States still remained.[6]

Industrialization did not change the process of collecting and preparing naval stores much over time; people still boxed trees well into the twentieth century. Industrialization only increased the demand for the products. Nonetheless, the division of labor played an important part in how the labor in the industry was managed. Boxcutters, dippers, kiln tenders, teamsters all had their separate skills. After emancipation, wages increased as a result of competition for labor. Luckily, demand increased along with costs, mostly as a result of new uses for naval stores. As late as 1921, a historian of this industry could write, "The progress of the wood turpentine industry is such as to justify the expectation that with each year, for some years to come, there will be an increase in its output and a ready market for the turpentine and rosin and other commodities supplied by it."[7] Spirits of turpentine became an important component in the rubber industry and in lamp oil. Rosin became a component in the manufacture of soap, floor covering, and lamp oil. These new uses were the result of industrialization, and the increase in production that they spurred had a devastating effect upon the environment where longleaf pine had once been located. In other words, the primary effect of industrialization on this environment was caused by demand, not supply.

Eventually, the industry came to realize that the number of trees available to tap and sometimes harvest (as there was a southern lumber industry too) was finite. The lumber companies could not move south forever. Recognition of these limits is what kept demand generated by the industrialization of other industries at a manageable rate. New methods were gradually developed that allowed for the harvesting of gum without destroying the tree. New efforts were made to protect trees from fire. Some producers allowed their trees to "rest" for years at a time before cutting new boxes on them. The longleaf pine could reproduce itself when producers exercised reasonable care. Increasingly, longleaf pines were kept on pine plantations where their growth and regrowth could be closely monitored. These developments fit into the wider effort known as the conservation movement. That meant limiting environmental destruction while still allowing industry to exploit natural resources. Industrialization also began to spur efforts that tended to resemble modern environmentalism, forcing industry to stop, or at least change its ways, because the damage it created could not be reversed or was too much of a burden for society to bear.

Industrialization and the Origins of American Environmentalism

Around the same time that some people began to recognize that the destruction of the longleaf pine ecosystem was irreversible and that some of the trees ought to be preserved, some people in California were beginning to make a new, non-industrial argument on behalf of the native redwoods and sequoias. Since nature could heal the mental wounds caused by industrialization, the trees had to be preserved for everyone's sake. "I chance to think of the thousands needing rest—the weary in soul and limb," wrote the naturalist John Muir in 1875. "The hall and the theater and the church have been invented, and compulsory education. Why not add compulsory recreation?"[8] Certainly, America's many neurasthenia sufferers would have benefited by the recuperative powers of these majestic places. Since so many sufferers of that particular disease were affluent, many of them likely did.

Unfortunately for this large population of potential campers, these particular trees were useful for making buildings. In 1850 old-growth forests covered about 2 million acres in the American West, mostly in California. By 1900 about one-third of that area had been cleared.[9] At first the industry depended upon huge squadrons of loggers to cut and process so many trees. With the development of steam power (which was, ironically, fueled by consuming still more wood), the trees disappeared even faster. They might have disappeared faster still had it not been for the efforts of early environmentalists like Muir. While Muir attracted a following with such pronouncements, he was part of a small minority. Most Americans saw forests and land as resources to fuel industrial growth rather than as unique places worthy of preservation.

It is tempting to blame the desire for unrestricted resource exploitation on greedy corporations, but in truth the idea that nature existed for people to exploit to the utmost had support from Americans of all social classes. Quickly extracting the resources from unsettled land was a prime path to wealth in late nineteenth-century America, and to limit the freedom to do that threatened the possibility of social mobility. Over time, however, it became increasingly clear that large corporations were the best suited to profitably extract the resources upon which industrialization depended. That is why it took until after the turn of the century for any kind of environmental regulation to find popular support. By then the benefits of industrialization were shared less equitably and the costs upon the environment were obvious to all. The creation of America's national park system was one legislative way to prevent the excesses of industrialization from destroying natural resources for all time. Antipollution legislation was another.

In many industrial cities around the turn of the twentieth century, pollution was considered a sign of progress. After all, if there was smoke coming out of the smokestacks, the factory had to be operating, and more smoke meant more output. Pueblo, Colorado, an industrial city in the Rocky Mountain West, was home to many kinds of industry, most notably a steel mill and numerous smelters where the product of local mines was refined into valuable precious metals. "Watch Pueblo's Smoke" was the motto of the local business association. One local booster who associated billowing smokestacks with prosperity described that smoke as a thing of beauty, "running from slate and deep blue, on through opalescent gray to chrome yellow and rich red."[10] Those Coloradoans forced to live near the toxic by-products that smelters produced were more inclined to see

The polluted air in Pittsburgh—home to steel mills and many other industrial plants
—became a symbol of the damage that unregulated industrial production could do
to the environment. *(Courtesy of the Library of Congress)*

the waste product of the state's main industry as a hazard to their health,
rather than a thing of beauty. The poor inhabitants of Denver and Pueblo
were not miners, but many of them paid with their health for the mining
industry's prosperity.

Working-class people who worked in polluting industries supported
their employers on the issue of pollution because they were more concerned with their jobs than the environment, even if a damaged environment threatened their health. After all, those effects were long-term
while unemployment was immediate. A committee of railway workers
defended their employer, the Illinois Central, and themselves in 1909:
"Smoke is at the present time an absolutely essential feature of industry,
of work and the advancement of civilization. Before smoke is suppressed
by law it must, in all justice, be proved that this can be done without
loss and without injury to the work that smoke now accomplishes."[11]
This kind of cross-class alliance was the result of mutual self-interest,
since, unlike on the question of wages, for example, when labor won,
management won too.

That is why the first environmental reformers were members of the
urban professional classes whose livelihoods were not tied directly to
profits from manufacturing. These reformers, many of them women,

did not offer a critique of industrial civilization in order to motivate the passage of legislation to make smoke go away. Instead, they attacked the notion that smoke equaled progress without attacking the notion of progress itself. They championed the idea that a beautiful city was a clean city. "A filthy city cannot be beautiful," opined the *Chicago Record-Herald* in 1911. "Smoke, soot and cinders render every attempt at adornment a hollow mockery."[12] Others, arguing that a smoky factory was not an efficient factory, encouraged new ways to power the engines that drove those factories instead of the cheap coal that powered so many steel mills and railroads.

Pittsburgh was once known as the smokiest city in America because its large industrial base was largely powered by the abundant but dirty anthracite coal deposits found just a short distance from town. "Pittsburg[h] is a smoky, dismal city at her best," noted one travel writer in 1884. "At her worst, nothing darker, dingier or more dispiriting could be imagined."[13] Living under these conditions affected not only every citizen's physical health but also their psychological well-being. Andrew Carnegie was so critical of the pollution that his mills helped to create that he moved to New York City, which was widely reputed to have the best air of any city in the country (perhaps because of its relative lack of large-scale factories). By the early twentieth century, Pittsburgh's antismoke crusaders included wealthy families like the Mellons. With no direct interest in iron, steel, or coal, they were more concerned about the environment than they were about the profits generated by those industries. Therefore, they financed scientific studies of pollution in western Pennsylvania that were eventually used to justify regulation.

Antismoke legislation, usually passed on the local level, is one of the least-remembered reforms of the Progressive Era. Pittsburgh passed its first antismoke ordinance in 1892, but it worked poorly since it only covered residential districts and exempted steel mills. A stronger smoke ordinance passed in 1907 as a result of public appeals regarding domestic cleanliness and the negative effect of pollution on the value of the city's real estate. Another common argument against air pollution was that the fuel contained in soot represented waste. The gradual shift from coal-fired steam power to electric power in western Pennsylvania's largest industries alleviated that problem by the 1920s. Probably because of such limited improvements, sustained and successful efforts at smoke control did not begin until the late 1930s. In 1871 a justice of the Pennsylvania Supreme Court described smoke as summing up "the characteristics of . . . [the] city, its kind of fuel, its business, the habits of its people and the industries which . . . [gave] it prosperity and wealth."[14] Today, with less heavy industry than ever, Pittsburgh's air quality no longer symbolizes its entire identity.

Environmental damage is a hard effect to lay entirely at the feet of industrialization. All economic growth requires resources. Industrialization simply meant that those resources were consumed faster than they might have been otherwise, particularly in terms of the supply of raw materials and the waste generated by the production process. Gradually, as Americans came to recognize the pressures that industry created, the notion of saving natural resources gave way to a consensus that they should be used more responsibly. Conservation promoted the efficient use of resources so that they would not be used up so quickly, especially resources like forests that were capable of renewing themselves if they were managed in a sustainable manner. As resources have become even scarcer over time, the environmental effects of industrialization have taken on an added significance since they have served as precedent for so much additional environmental damage to come. The ability of Americans to move from one region of the country often did a great deal to spread that damage.

Notes

1. Ronald M. Labbé and Jonathan Lurie, *The Slaughterhouse Cases: Regulation, Reconstruction and the Fourteenth Amendment* (Lawrence: University Press of Kansas, 2003), 6.
2. In Labbé and Lurie, 60.
3. *Slaughterhouse Cases*, 83 U.S. 36 (1873).
4. In Mark Kurlansky, *The Big Oyster: History on the Half Shell* (New York: Ballantine Books, 2006), 155.
5. In Shibu Jose, Erik J. Jokela, and Deborah L. Miller, "Introduction," in *The Longleaf Pine Ecosystem*, ed. Shibu Jose, Erik J. Jokela, and Deborah L. Miller (Boston: Springer, 2006), 24.
6. Jose et al., 4.
7. Thomas Gamble, *Naval Stores: History, Production, Distribution and Consumption* (Savannah: Review Publishing & Printing Co., 1921), 75.
8. In David G. Schuster, *Neurasthenic Nation: America's Search for Health, Happiness and Comfort, 1869–1920* (New Brunswick: Rutgers University Press, 2011), 137.
9. Andrew Isenberg, *Mining California: An Ecological History* (New York: Hill & Wang, 2005), 77.
10. In Thomas M. Andrews, *Killing for Coal: America's Deadliest Labor War* (Cambridge, MA: Harvard University Press, 2008), 66.

11. In David Stradling, *Smokestacks and Progressives: Environmentalists, Engineers and Air Quality in America, 1881–1951* (Baltimore: Johns Hopkins University Press, 1999), 123.

12. In Stradling, 25.

13. In Joel A. Tarr, "Some Thoughts About the Pittsburgh Environment," in *Devastation and Renewal: An Environmental History of Pittsburgh and Its Region*, ed. Joel A. Tarr (Pittsburgh: University of Pittsburgh Press, 2003), 3.

14. In Tarr, 114.

Transportation

Q. *How could manufacturers dispose of their surplus product?*

Railroads were America's first big businesses. The largest railroads were larger than any other businesses in America by a huge order of magnitude. They were also very expensive to build and maintain. Government investment was essential for completing such ventures. Over the course of fifty years, the railroads reoriented the American West from a region where most people traveled north and south to one where they traveled east or west. In doing so, the railroads made it possible to ship both people and goods of all kinds on a precise schedule. The administrative model that railroads provided also proved to be the inspiration for many entrepreneurs as they increased the scale of their businesses later in the century.

Railroads provided fast, regular, dependable all-weather transportation while simultaneously lowering the cost of transporting anything. They could also bring those goods to more precise locations since there no longer needed to be a waterway around to get transportation more efficient than a horse-drawn carriage. Many historians have remarked on the ability of railroads to compact spaces. Places that had once been separated by many days' journeys became much more accessible if the two cities were served by a railroad line. People, goods, and information all could move faster by rail. All these effects were transformative to American society, and they grew more transformative as railroads became increasingly efficient and more numerous.

The first railroads in America appeared during the 1820s. These operations were small by later standards and entirely regional, created primarily to supplement existing water transportation. When railroads became national in scale for the first time during the 1850s, they were totally nonstandardized, using different track gauges, parts, and the like. They did not even try to coordinate the movement of trains by using the telegraph lines that were often strung along their tracks until after the Civil War. Unable to negotiate all the different companies it took to move anything across the country, railroads organized themselves into cartels so as to facilitate fast freight trains that brought the natural resources of the West to the industrializing East and the people from the East to the unsettled lands beyond the Mississippi. Railroads helped integrate these people into streams of commerce that traveled throughout the world economy, bringing their farm products, meat, and minerals to markets all over the world. Building the infrastructure to make this possible took lots of time and money. Between 1873 and 1890, the total amount of freight carried on America's railroads increased from about 100 million to about 800 million pounds.[1] Between 1880 and 1916, total track mileage in the United States increased from 93,000 to 254,000 miles.[2] As the result of both these trends, the cost of shipping anything by rail dropped significantly, making goods produced in industrialized factories even more affordable.

A key milestone in America's industrial development was the completion of the first transcontinental railroad in 1869. To achieve such an extraordinary feat of engineering required millions of dollars in investment and thousands of men to build and supply both railroads—the Central Pacific building west to east and the Union Pacific building east to west. Each man had a particular task, just as he might have had if he were working in a factory. Once the first and other transcontinental railroads were completed, such companies advertised heavily to get people to migrate west, not just for the one-time price of a one-way ticket, but for the lifetime of business that their commerce could provide, especially if they were farmers. In the case of the Central Pacific and the Union Pacific, both railroads also had land to sell to these new settlers, land that had been given to them by the United States government in exchange for their efforts.

Before these two railroads joined up at Promentory Point, Utah, traveling from New York to San Francisco could take months and as much as $1,000. With the transcontinental railroad complete, that journey took seven days (with stops) and could cost as little as $65.[3] This decrease in cost, both for people and for freight, had enormous economic effects. As the editor Samuel Bowles noted long before the first transcontinental railroad was even completed, "To feel the importance of the Pacific [R]ailroad . . . you must come across the mountains to the Pacific Coast. There you will see half a continent waiting for its vivifying influences.

You will witness a boundless agriculture, fickle and hesitating for lack of the regular markets this would give. You will find mineral wealth immeasurable, locked up, wastefully worked, or gambled away, until this shall open to it abundant labor, cheap capital, wood, water, oversight, steadiness of production,—everything that makes mining a certainty and not a chance."[4] As Bowles predicted, Western industry flourished in the years following the opening of the railroad. Since railroads provided a means to take huge amounts of food to market, industrialized, single-crop farming was in a sense the product of the railroad too.

The initial costs of building a transcontinental railroad were extraordinary. The costs of operating a railroad of any significant size were extraordinary as well. The money needed to build any line only increased if the terrain was unfriendly. Therefore such railroads required not only the backing of large investors, but concessions from the government in order to survive. Despite the lucrative goods they carried to market, many lines resorted to collusion in order to stay afloat. Big lines took over smaller lines since buying out competitors proved more effective than merely trusting them. The lack of meaningful government regulation allowed the railroads to often charge as much as the market could possibly bear. Despite tremendous power and extraordinary government support, railroads often failed as businesses. For example, hundreds of lines went bankrupt during the Panic of 1893, including the Northern Pacific, the Union Pacific, and the Santa Fe railroads.

During normal times, those firms that shipped their goods to market by rail were willing to pay what they had to because no other way existed for big companies to expand their markets. Railroads also became the biggest employers in America. Since many of their employees were skilled, they were more likely to unionize. The Great Railroad Strike of 1877 and the Pullman Strike of 1894 stand as testaments both to the difficulties unions faced and the importance of railroads to the functioning of the economy since both these far-reaching disputes ground the entire American railroad system to a halt.

Railroads were not a disruptive technology as much as they were a technology that facilitated the disruptive effects of other production processes. Cheaper transportation costs, like cheaper manufacturing costs, meant lower prices, and lower prices meant that industries of all kinds were threatened by the spread of railroads. Industrialized businesses that operated on a grand scale could expand their markets by shipping on railroads. Small-scale businesses could not afford to grow when they had to compete against cheaper goods shipped in from elsewhere. As industrialization progressed, the existing order of things adapted to the new economic realities that industrialized transportation facilitated. The prices of goods became cheaper, but the effects of these transportation changes were not all positive.

The Power of the Locomotive

Railroads not only facilitated industrialization when finished, but the resources it took to build them spurred industrialization too. For example, railroads required lumber for their tracks and steel for their cars and their engines. Nowhere is the industrial process needed to build a railroad more apparent than in the locomotive, a universal symbol of the new age. The Baldwin Locomotive Works was the largest locomotive builder in the world during the late nineteenth and early twentieth centuries. Its factories covered eight and a half acres over seven city blocks near downtown Philadelphia, Pennsylvania. Its product was sold worldwide. When a Japanese delegation visited America in 1872 in order to see the progress of American industrial society, the Baldwin Locomotive Works was the first such site they visited.

The Baldwin Locomotive Works serves as a good example of a facet of industrialization that is poorly remembered today: the capital equipment sector. The American model of industrialization was generally to build as many units as possible of something, and then sell as many of them as possible for the lowest possible price. The capital equipment sector worked on a different model. Baldwin produced a few hundred specimens of large expensive goods each year. While the company maintained many patterns upon which to base the design of those locomotives, each one was essentially made to order, designed to meet the operational needs of the railroad that ordered it. Most product manufacturers generally built their product, then marketed and sold it. Industrial builders like the Baldwin Locomotive Works generally did the exact opposite.

Despite having a starkly different business model from other firms described up to this point in this book, Baldwin made use of the same principles of mechanization and the division of labor upon which manufacturers using the more common model of industrialization depended. The firm employed countless skilled workers—markers, drillers, rollers, flangers, riveters, chippers, caulkers, and their helpers—to perform the painstaking work that went into many parts of the finished products.

Each worker would perform a particular function on a semifinished locomotive, and then move on to the next one. Other workers used machine tools driven by electric motors and high-speed steel-cutting tools. Thanks to such innovations, an experiment in 1889 demonstrated that the works could build a working locomotive out of raw materials in just eight working days.

Despite the custom-built nature of railroad engines, Baldwin still incorporated other developments related to industrialization into its production process over the course of the late nineteenth century in order to improve the efficiency of its operations. In 1850 most of Baldwin's skilled workers depended on hand tools to cut and shape the metal coming from the company's furnaces. Over time the company added power tools to bore holes and shave planes. The firm also changed its organizational structure in order to produce standardized parts for its customized products. Every model of locomotive was still made to order, but often the same part could be used for any number of designs. This kind of production process demonstrated that the Baldwin Works valued both flexibility and efficiency. It allowed the works to greatly increase its output to fill the demand created by all the new railroads in America. By the mid-1870s the Baldwin works branched out to produce steam-powered streetcars for the first time.

Not only were locomotives and the passenger cars that followed them produced in an industrial manner, riding on a railroad was another way to benefit from industrialization besides purchasing the end products of that process. Traveling by railroad highlighted the difference between benefiting from and actually operating a machine. Passengers did not have to do anything to get where they were going. They simply sat back and let the machine do the work. Travel inside a railroad car made weather irrelevant and almost eliminated the need to consider the terrain (except for what you saw looking out the window). Like factories, locomotives ran on steam power (even if the engines they used were quite different). Locomotives could consume unprecedented amounts of fuel very quickly. They did so in order to be able to haul large loads for great lengths of time. Their travels increased the flow of resources bound for factories and the flow of factory products bound for distant markets, thereby greatly increasing the economic impact of industrialization. However, the general public was much more likely to recognize the locomotive, rather than the products it carried, as a symbol of industrialization, which meant that trains inevitably entered the public consciousness.

The symbolic power of the locomotive was obvious to those for whom railroad travel was relatively new. Charles Francis Adams Jr.—grandson and great-grandson of former United States presidents—despite being a railroad executive, still experienced the sense of wonder that trains could produce, most notably from the powerful locomotives that led them. "It is but necessary to stand once on the platform of a way station and to look at an express train dashing by," he wrote in 1876. "There are few sights finer; few better-calculated to quicken the pulses. It is most striking at night. The glare of the headlight, the rush and throb of the locomotive, the connecting rod and driving wheels which seem instinct with nervous life, the flashing lamps in the cars, and the final whirl of dust in which the red tail lights vanish almost as soon as they are seen—all this is well calculated to excite our wonder."[5] The locomotive was also the subject of two Walt Whitman poems.

Because railroads could not have been built or operated properly without the assistance of the government, especially the federal government, the locomotive also had political significance. To the novelist Frank Norris, it was "the galloping monster, the terror of steel and steam, with its single eye, cyclopean, red, shooting from horizon to horizon . . . the symbol of vast power, huge, terrible, flinging the echo of its thunder all over the reaches of the valley, leaving blood and destruction in its path."[6] Unlike Adams, the farmers that Norris wrote about had no control over the rates they had to pay to send their products to market. They were dependent upon, not beneficiaries of, the power of the steam engine. Even today, when railroads are no longer an important means of transportation for most Americans, many people remain fascinated by trains, perhaps because they still suggest a mastery of time and space that is difficult to appreciate without remembering the changes that came during the late nineteenth century.

Railroad Space, Railroad Time

It seems ridiculous to suggest that railroads could change time, but that is precisely what they did in both the figurative and literal senses. The figurative sense refers most obviously to travel times. When a railroad line connected two cities, the travel time between them dropped significantly since it was so much easier to get there by rail than by foot or by horse. Thus a city that was many miles away from a central point but connected by the railroad was more easily accessible and seemed "closer" than a city that was geographically nearer but not served by the railroad line. Changing time in this manner accelerated commerce along railway lines. Total goods shipped by railroad increased eleven times over during this era. By 1900 almost everything people used or wanted in their daily lives traveled to them via railroad. Locations not along railroad lines seemed distant, even if they were physically close to central cities.

Railroads were obsessed with speed from the very beginning. Tracks were laid out over the most direct routes possible in order to save construction time even if those routes contained steep grades and hairpin turns as a result. Not hours but days were shaved off travel distances between cities as railroads replaced steamboats and carriages as the main mode of passenger transportation in America. After the invention of the Westinghouse airbrake in 1869, loaded trains could stop more easily. Rather than accept the safety benefit that the airbrake bestowed, railroads just ran heavier trains faster. As a result of this long-standing attitude, horrible accidents on railroads were common. In 1904, for example, a bridge collapse near Eden, Colorado, led to the drowning of 88 people. In 1907 there were 8,026 train collisions somewhere in America.[7]

Railroads also literally changed time by affecting the way that people set their clocks. Railroads had to operate on a regular schedule. In the early days, when they ran on only one track, irregular scheduling could lead to head-on crashes if two trains came upon each other from opposite directions. In the era of industrialization, regularity was also imposed upon them by their customers. Trains had to run whether they were full or not because they were needed at their destination point to make their next trip. Trains "go and come with such regularity and precision," wrote Henry David Thoreau, "that the farmers set their clocks by them, and thus one well-conducted institution regulates a whole country."[8] This was just the most obvious manifestation of the extraordinary power of railroads to influence daily life in America. Other changes in daily routines were more subtle. The main meal during the nineteenth century had once been dinner, a large repast served during the afternoon, followed by supper in the evening. As factories forced employees to stay through the day or, in the case of upper-class workers who lived in the suburbs, made it impossible for them to make it home for dinner and return to work, what they ate in the evening became the larger meal.

Before the railroads came along, every city in America kept time by the sun. That system meant different times in different cities, depending upon the position of the sun in each of them. Noon was always when the sun was directly overhead. While these discrepancies were fine in an economy where few people traveled more than twenty miles from their home in their entire lifetime, they were not conducive to a system of nationwide commerce. Boats, steamships, and road vehicles, dependent upon forces that they could not entirely predict, tended to be imprecise, but people had to know that they could make their connecting trains. In 1882 the American Society of Civil Engineers reported, "Mistakes in the hour of the day are frequent. In every city or town, in every State, discrepancies are met which produce aggregate inconvenience. Thousands of engagements are broken. Innumerable disappointments and losses result."[9] By the 1850s mass-produced pocket watches allowed people to keep time well enough to follow the industrial rhythms that railroads promoted. By the mid-1870s American firms, using machinery for many tasks, could produce watches that undersold Swiss imports, yet still matched their foreign competition in quality.

Now that nearly every American could know immediately what time it was, the way Americans kept the time needed to be organized. During the middle of the nineteenth century, most railroads kept time on the basis of the time in the city where their headquarters were located. Railroad stations, therefore, often kept two clocks: one for local time, another for railroad time. Around the country, there were at least fifty-three different time standards. In 1869, a teacher named Samuel Dowd laid out a system of four time zones in America, each an hour apart. In 1883 all of North America's railroads agreed to follow that system—essentially the same time zone system still in place today. People protested that this was somehow unnatural. "Damn Vanderbilt's time!" exclaimed one critic, referring to a major owner of many eastern railroads. "We want God's time!"[10] Significant tensions came with the imposition of railroad time. As George Beard noted in *American Nervousness*, "We are under constant strain, mostly unconscious . . . to get somewhere or do something at some definite moment."[11] Pittsburgh banned the railroad time zones until 1887. The United States government did not endorse the time zone system until 1918. Resistance was not based just on the fact that this maneuver altered the relationship between people and nature; it also seemed fundamentally undemocratic. After all, who elected the railroads to determine what time it should be? Yet railroad time soon became the only accepted time, thereby saving everyone the trouble of keeping multiple clocks.

The efficiency and precision that railroad time reflects were the values of an industrial society. Railroads were a symbol of speed and progress.

The railroads depended on industrial rhythms so the railroads helped make those rhythms the rhythms of the entire society. Coordinating the vast flows of goods inside and across different railroad networks was the primary purpose of railroad managers. Without standardized times and new forms of accounting, railroads would not have been nearly as profitable. As they had very high fixed costs, railroads had to keep freight cars as full as possible on every leg of many long journeys. This required the kind of precise scheduling that only good record keeping and exact timekeeping could ensure. As a result, a flood of manufactured goods, produced by methods developed during the Civil War and transported by a newly national railway system, helped mend a country that had broken apart. Railroads transported not only goods, but information about the wider world to places that would have had trouble getting it by any other means.

Steamships

Most of the products of American industrialization went to other parts of America during this era. Even during the decade after 1920, foreign commerce never constituted more than 10 percent of the value of the country's total goods and services. This explains why railroads were undoubtedly the most important new means of transportation during the era of industrialization, but they were not the only one. Lines like the Pennsylvania Railroad got involved in the steamship business early on so that they could provide their customers and goods with seamless travel between the American interior and points overseas. These efforts were often money losing propositions, since the fixed costs of operating a steamship were high and this industry was dominated by British interests like the Cunard Line. They had begun to replace wind-powered packet ships earlier in the century, cutting the travel time between England and America from a matter of months to a matter of weeks.

For much of the nineteenth century, the British and the Germans primarily controlled trans-Atlantic steamship traffic. The United States only began to assert itself in this market during the 1880s as its ship-building industry became heavily industrialized. The steamships of the late nineteenth century were the most complicated creations of the era of industrialization. Their construction required industrial know-how, but they were far too big to be mass-produced. The construction of a steamship resembled the construction of a steam locomotive in that it

Steamships, like the *Egypt* and *Spain* depicted here, were both the products of industrialization and a boon to industrialization because they transported so many immigrant workers to the United States. *(Courtesy of the Library of Congress)*

required enormous amounts of trial and error to find the perfect combination of the proper scale and the best design to make a ship built to that scale run as efficiently as possible. Steam propelled these ships. It also heated the rooms, heated the food, and might even run the tools in the onboard barber shop. The invention of the Bessemer process allowed steamships to be built of steel for the first time, making them both lighter and stronger than the iron ships that they replaced. While steel was more expensive than iron, it was also lighter, which ultimately saved on fuel costs if the ship made enough journeys.

Steamships carried many things across oceans in both directions. One was people. Emigrants from Europe became immigrants when they landed in New York. Competition between the steamship lines became so fierce that it eventually became possible to emigrate to America for a ten-dollar ticket. While the rich traveled in luxury, poor immigrants, who had to scrape together the accumulated savings of years in order to buy even the cheapest ticket, often traveled in overcrowded squalor. To meet the spike in passengers that industrialization in America encouraged, steamship lines packed passengers into steerage under alarming conditions. "Sweeping is the only form of cleaning done," explained a report from the United States Immigration Commission. "No sick cans are furnished, and not even large receptacles for waste. The vomitings of the sick are often permitted to remain a long time before being removed. The floors, when iron, are continually damp, and when wood they reek with foul odor because they are not washed."[12] Bad weather or an accident (like the *Titanic* hitting that iceberg) would, of course, affect everyone on board, but only the poor risked dying from disease because of these temporary conditions.

Not all steamships carried passengers for profit. Steamships were largely responsible for the first globalized food chains, since they could carry grain or fruit in their holds just as well as they could carry people. After the technology of refrigerated shipping was perfected, the international meat trade proved very profitable to both the producers and the shippers. It should not be surprising that exporters concentrated their efforts upon making it viable to trade such a high-value foodstuff first. This required the successful utilization of mechanical refrigeration on shipboard. From there it found many other uses for this technology because beef exports by ocean-going vessels proved so immediately successful.

The first shipments of American beef to Great Britain came during the mid-1870s. Alarm from English ranchers was immediately palpable in the press. American beef captured 94 percent of the British market between 1880 and 1889, its most successful period.[13] The immediate reason that American beef captured the English market so quickly was not just its price, but its quality. This was a function of the technology that preserved it. American producers kept their beef chilled rather than frozen for the comparatively short voyage across the Atlantic. Freezing affects the physical structure of meat, making it less moist. It can also rupture small blood vessels in the muscle fiber, making it look less appetizing. Most domestic English beef, on the other hand, seemed scraggy by comparison. Salted or canned beef, another alternative, simply could not compare to fresh meat and quickly became the exclusive province of consumers who could not afford the fresher kinds.

The successful application of mechanical refrigeration on ships led to improvements in mechanical refrigeration on land too. Many kinds of refrigerating machines were developed for cold storage, brewing, and fruit importation. Even nonfood-related industries like rubber manufacturing and gunpowder production benefited from the solutions to technological problems with mechanical refrigeration that were first worked out on shipboard. These successes, of course, were the direct precursor to the multinational, globalized food chains of today. Those, in turn, have had a direct effect upon the diet of every person in the industrialized world. While refrigeration has little to do with transportation technology, it does demonstrate how the kinds of technologies worked out during the development of industrialized transportation had application across many other industries. Government regulation not only affected how transportation systems operated, but also had the capacity to affect how every aspect of the industrialized economy operated. Yet government seldom even tried to wield its potential power. The next chapter tries to explain why.

Notes

1. Richard White, *Railroaded: The Transcontinentals and the Making of Modern America* (New York W.W. Norton, 2011), 523.

2. John F. Stover, "Railroads," *The Reader's Companion to American History*, ed. Eric Foner and John A. Garraty (Boston: Houghton Mifflin, 1991), 908.

3. Stephen E. Ambrose, *Nothing Like It in the World: The Men Who Built the Transcontinental Railroad, 1863–1869* (New York: Touchstone, 2000), 369.

4. Samuel Bowles, *Across the Continent: A Summer's Journey to the Rocky Mountains.* (New York: Hurd & Houghton, 1866), 255.

5. Charles Francis Adams Jr., *Notes on Railroad Accidents* (New York: G.P. Putnam's Sons, 1879), 269.

6. Frank Norris, *The Octopus* (New York: Penguin, 1994, originally published 1901), 51.

7. Mark Aldrich, *Death Rode the Rails: American Railroad Accidents and Safety, 1828–1965* (Baltimore: Johns Hopkins University Press, 2006), 182.

8. Henry David Thoreau, *Walden; or, Life* in *the Woods* in *Thoreau* (New York: Library of America, 1985), 416.

9. In Alan Trachtenberg, *The Incorporation of America: Culture and Society in the Gilded Age* (New York: Hill & Wang, 2007), 60.

10. In Jack Beatty, *Age of Betrayal: The Triumph of Money in America, 1865–1900* (New York: Alfred A. Knopf, 2007), 5.

11. George M. Beard, *American Nervousness: Its Causes and Consequences* (New York: G.P. Putnam's Sons, 1881), 104.

12. United States Immigration Commission, *Reports of the Immigration Commission: Steerage Conditions* (Washington, DC: Government Printing Office, 1911), 7.

13. David M. Higgins and Dev Gangjee, "'Trick or Treat?': The Misrepresentation of American Beef Exports in Britain during the Late Nineteenth Century," *Enterprise and Society* 11 (June 2010): 209.

The Politics of
Industrialization

Q. *Why didn't the political system do more
to limit the excesses of industrialization?*

In 1914 a young journalist named Walter Lippmann wrote an extraordinarily prescient book about the American political system called *Drift and Mastery*. While the book was nominally about the time at which Lippmann wrote it, many of the principles that Lippmann outlined apply just as well to American politics now as they did then. Nowhere is this truer than with respect to the two concepts in Lippmann's title. By "mastery," Lippmann meant the efforts of the American political system to master the economic forces unleashed by changes in the production and distribution of goods. Democracy, in other words, had to be used to tame the excesses of industrialization. As Lippmann explained it, "Politics is becoming the chief method by which the consumer enforces his interests upon the industrial system."[1] Unfortunately, Lippmann also saw that the political system had been overwhelmed by the sheer extent of the economic changes during that era. The government could not (or would not) pass the legislation needed to make the industrial system respond to the popular will.

That is where the word "drift" comes in. Lippmann defined drift as what happens when government does nothing to assuage the costs of such transformative economic changes. While government, and to some extent society, drifted along aimlessly, a small group of determined industrialists forced changes upon the majority of Americans that made their lives worse. The industrialists called it "progress" and they convinced most people to measure that progress in material goods. "Men look at the industrial world to-day, and find it produces enormous quantities of goods," Lippmann wrote. "They reason that any change would result in the production of less goods. That is the logic of their fear."[2] Lippmann lamented the fact that impoverished Americans had no stake in this progress and no "taste of its promise."[3] The benefits of industrialization bypassed its victims, but those victims could not make the political system represent their interests. As a result, corporate activity powered along mostly unregulated.

Although the people disrupted by industrialization lamented the failure of the political system to look out for their interests, industrialists and their supporters came up with a number of ideological justifications for unfettered capitalism. The most important of these ideologies came to be known as Social Darwinism. Charles Darwin published his theory of evolution in his 1859 classic, *On the Origin of Species*. According to Darwin's theory, the process by which evolution worked was natural selection, the survival of the fittest. Darwin's theory caused a sensation, and not only among people who refused to believe that humans descended from apes. The British philosopher Herbert Spencer (who actually coined the phrase "survival of the fittest") and the American philosopher William Graham Sumner took Darwin's theory and applied it to human beings. The implication of this theory was that those who were rich were somehow superior to ordinary folk because they were able to work their way up to that position. Society then rewarded the fittest people with wealth and success. Any effort to penalize that success through higher taxes or government regulation of their business activities was therefore "unnatural."

Another justification for an unregulated system was the concept of "laissez-faire," from the French for "let alone." As befitting a French term, it originated with French political economists during the eighteenth century. Its original meaning connoted an economy in which an enterprise did not have to obtain a charter from the state in order to conduct business, a requirement that was common at that time. The term "laissez-faire" became popular in America during the era of industrialization with a different meaning. Industrialists and their supporters defined it as an economy without government interference of any kind, which meant they could use this concept to justify keeping as much of the proceeds of their business activities as they possibly could. Therefore, as the British observer James Bryce explained in his 1889 study of the United States political system, *The American Commonwealth*, "The functions of government must be kept at their minimum."[4] While this ideal may sound good in theory, it never existed in fact, even before the development of an activist government in the United States during the 1930s.

The same industrialists who emphasized the importance of eliminating government interference in the economy during the era of industrialization benefited mightily from government interference in the economy on behalf of their interests. Most notably, the high tariffs of this era (taxes on imported goods) limited competition from abroad for the goods that so many of them produced. The McKinley Tariff of 1890, for example (named after its author, the future president William McKinley), was directed precisely at those goods for which foreign competition was the steepest. The duty on tin plate, for example, which was used for room shingles and the manufacture of tin cans—an industry that did not exist in the United States at the time of its passage—was more than doubled. In order to get around that tariff, a new domestic tin plate industry quickly emerged. At the same time, the tariff on sugar was cut in order to make it more affordable to consumers and to reduce the federal government's large surplus. Only after World War I did America become productive enough that politicians worried as much about opening up foreign markets as they did about protecting domestic ones.

On the local level, corrupt political machines served as a rudimentary welfare state in order to cushion the damage that industrialization did. If your family did not earn enough money for a Christmas turkey, the machine would provide you one in exchange for your vote. If your dumb relative needed a job, the machine would employ the otherwise unemployable. Unlike middle-class urban reformers, the machine stood as a bulwark against Prohibition, a notion that was totally alien to many of their immigrant constituents. In fact, a common place to meet your local alderman was a nearby tavern. Many machine politicians were tavern owners by trade. George Washington Plunkitt, an operative in New York City's Tammany Hall machine, argued that "when a man works in politics, he should get something out of it." Most poor people agreed with him because they got something out of politics too.[5]

Another sign of drift was the ability of industrial interests to repurpose the federal government to their own ends. The administration of President Ulysses S. Grant was notoriously corrupt, rife with payments to public officials by companies in search of business or favors from the government. The notorious "whiskey rings" of that era involved federal officials in many cities getting kickbacks for themselves and for the Republican Party in exchange for distillers avoiding paying excise taxes. These kinds of scandals gave rise to demands for the end of what was known as the spoils system, the process by which the winner of the presidential election got to appoint his choices to nearly every federal job available. The beginning of the end of this practice came with the Pendleton Civil

Taverns were not just places where tired industrial workers relaxed, they were centers of political activity in places like New York City. *(Courtesy of the Library of Congress)*

Service Reform Act of 1883, which was supposed to make government work more effectively by removing federal appointments from the control of either party and instituting a professional bureaucracy instead. Unfortunately, that law affected only 10 percent of the federal workforce when first passed. While more federal government offices would become nonpartisan over time, persistent government corruption tended to accentuate the power of corporations rather than limit it.

The Sherman Antitrust Act

Industrialization led to the growth of large businesses because they were best suited to take advantage of this phenomenon. This was in large part the result of the economies of scale, which encouraged large companies to exploit their efficiencies in order to take control of markets in goods of all kinds. In 1865 no single firm in the United States was worth $10 million. In 1904 America had 300 such firms. These firms owned over 40 percent of the country's entire industrial wealth.[6] Many of these large companies were organized as trusts. The term "trust" refers to the manner in which many large companies were organized, but was used generally to apply to any company with a huge share of the market for a particular good it produced. One observer joked around the turn of the twentieth century that Americans were born to benefit the milk trust and died to benefit the coffin trust. (Indeed, there really was a coffin trust, organized by the banker J.P. Morgan in 1898.)

Based on the principles of common law, the Sherman Antitrust Act of 1890 was designed to combat the negative effects of the natural growth of companies due to the economies of scale that industrialization cultivated. The law came about as a result of the first organized monopolies in the United States, which were perceived as a threat to American freedom— not just economic freedom, but the freedom of Americans to live in comfort the way that industrialization made possible. Not all trusts were monopolies, but the two terms were often used interchangeably for firms that seemed to be reaping all the benefits of industrialization for themselves by limiting the effects of competition that kept prices down and allowed more people to partake of the goods and services they created. The Sherman Act was designed to protect tariffs like McKinley's. By preventing monopolies from forming and wielding too much power—the thinking went—the law ensured that tariffs would be set for the benefit of the country as a whole rather than manufacturers in particular. While this equation worked on a political level, whether the act actually achieved this goal was open to question.

The key part of the Sherman Act read, "Every contract, combination in the form of trust or otherwise, or conspiracy, in restraint of trade or commerce among the several States, or with foreign nations, is hereby declared to be illegal."[7] Such language, like all aspects of the common law, is overly general. However, the law allowed the enforcement of the law to adapt to changing economic circumstances over time. The only punishment specified in the act was a small fine. The Sherman Antitrust Act was hardly ever employed during the 1890s. Only later did the government employ the law to dissolve monopolies. Many business leaders, even after the turn of the twentieth century, believed that monopolies were the inevitable result of free market capitalism since very large companies benefited most from new technologies. If that new technology allowed them to lower the price of the goods they produced, then the public benefited too. However, a significant opposition to monopolies arose because many monopolies did not behave that way. It was unreasonable to believe that many small stockholders could organize themselves so as to prevent the companies they owned from acting against the public interest, assuming they even wanted to do so. Therefore, the government was justified in stepping in and controlling the monopolies' behavior.

Unfortunately, as Lippmann noted in *Drift and Mastery*, many corporations had grown stronger than the government. Monopolies grew beyond the reach of the law and existed despite the law. This became possible because the Sherman Antitrust Act was often misused. For the first ten years after its passage, the law was primarily employed against labor unions, even though Senator John Sherman, the author of the act, had specifically stated that this was not his intention. In 1894 the Supreme Court refused to apply the Sherman Act to the sugar monopoly, the E.C. Knight Company, even though it controlled 98 percent of the market in that product. That decision sent a message to corporations that they could essentially combine at will. Between 1895 and 1904 America went through what would become known as the great merger movement. Over the course of those years, thousands of firms disappeared by getting absorbed into other companies. At the end of this process, one or two giant companies controlled over half the market of seventy-eight distinct industries.[8] By limiting competition through mergers, their new corporate parents were able to keep more of the financial benefits of industrialization to themselves.

The merger movement ended in large part because President Theodore Roosevelt was willing to distinguish between good trusts and bad trusts. He believed that the Northern Securities Company, a holding company resulting from the merger of the main railroads in the northwestern United States, was one of the bad ones. Therefore, he directed Philander Knox, his attorney general, to file suit against it in an effort to break it apart because of its deleterious effect upon commerce. By 1904 the United States Supreme Court was also willing to employ the Sherman Act as it was originally intended. In *Northern Securities Co. v. United States*, the court not only agreed that the holding company at the heart of the case should be dissolved, but upheld the constitutionality of the Sherman Act for the first time. However, the result of the case did not really change the way the railroads that Northern Securities managed were operated. Regulated competition, Knox explained, would "show even greater common benefits" than before.[9] In 1910, for example, the Supreme Court approved of the breakup of John D. Rockefeller's Standard Oil trust, arguing that its actions had "unduly" restrained trade. Ironically, the stock of the separate companies soon doubled in overall value, making Rockefeller twice as rich as he was before the breakup of Standard Oil.

While the Sherman Antitrust Act did not fundamentally affect the control of large corporations over the economy, it did suggest that capitalism had its limits. The principle behind the Sherman Act (if not its execution) did signal a new direction by the government to redirect more of the benefits of industrialization away from companies and toward the public at large. "The combination here in question may have been for the pecuniary benefit of those who formed or caused it to be formed," explained Justice John Marshall Harlan in his majority opinion in the *Northern Securities* case. "But the interests of private persons and corporations cannot be made paramount to the interests of the general public."[10] The Sherman Act also served as precedent for future government intervention in the economy for the benefit of consumers and workers.

The constitutional justification for this was the Constitution's commerce clause, the same justification offered by the Court in the *Northern Securities* case. Therefore, Congress passed the Clayton Antitrust Act in 1914 to clarify its intentions on this subject. A key clause in that law stated that the "labor of a human being is not a commodity or article of commerce," thereby eliminating the possibility of antitrust prosecutions against unions. The use of the commerce clause in this manner set an important precedent for the policies of President Franklin D. Roosevelt's New Deal. While they are not always enforced the way reformers would like, the United States continues to have the strictest antimonopoly laws in the world down to this day.

Populism

With the political system essentially broken, it is no wonder that many groups had made efforts to reform it from the outside. These included antimonopolists, greenbackers (who supported currency not backed by precious metals), prohibitionists (who supported the outlawing of the manufacture and distribution of alcoholic beverages), and various attempts at labor parties. Considering these unsuccessful efforts by groups directly victimized by industrialization, it may be surprising to some that the first sustained effort at wholesale political reform during the late nineteenth century in America was based in rural states and conducted mostly by farmers. The common thread for all these groups was concern about the power of the vast fortunes that were being accumulated by such a small number of winners in American society. For decades, agrarian reformers had been denouncing the exploitative practices of American railroads and the high tariffs that made it more difficult for farmers to sell their crops overseas. Much of this earlier discontent got sidetracked by the ability of midwestern and southern farmers to resettle on new lands under the terms of the Homestead Act of 1863. While this option remained open even after the frontier had supposedly closed, other farmers were saddled by debt, much of it incurred when they bought the machinery needed to work large farms. As a result of such problems, disgruntled farmers turned to politics in order to find a solution.

In 1892 the leaders of grassroots farmers' organizations known as the Farmer's Alliances created a new political party, the People's Party, soon to be better known as the Populist Party. A close look at Populist ideology shows that much of its rhetoric was anti-industrial. As one Minnesota farmer reasoned in 1891, "I settled on this land in good faith; built house and farm . . . Spent years of hard grubbing, fencing and improving. Are they going to drive us out like trespassers . . . and give us away to the Corporations? How can they support them when we are robbed of our means? . . . We must decay and die from woe and sorrow."[11] Populists also exhibited a common American paranoia, based on the notion that various unnamed "interests" were conspiring against them. The Populist organizer Mary Lease told farmers in her standard stump speech, "The great common people of this country are slaves, and monopoly is the master. The West and South are bound and prostrate before the manufacturing East."[12] To Populists the differences between the two major parties on issues like the tariff were mostly a sham.

Such comments reflect the regional tensions in the country at this time. The agricultural areas in the West and South had different interests than the East. For instance, high tariffs (taxes on imported goods) helped manufacturers who wanted to avoid competition with foreign goods, but crippled farmers who wanted to sell their excess product in foreign markets. Unfortunately for farmers, the eastern manufacturing interests controlled the government. The goal of the Populist Party was to create a government that was responsive to the farmers' concerns, rather than the concerns of industrialists interested in developing an international market through high tariffs and expensive credit. "From the same prolific

While Democrats feared that William Jennings Bryan's populist message would swallow the entire party, in fact the Bryan-led Democratic Party swallowed the Populist Party by co-opting part of its economic message. *(Courtesy of the Library of Congress)*

womb of government injustice we breed the two great classes—tramps and millionaires," argued the Omaha Platform of 1892, the Populists' first platform as a political party.[13] With some political success that year, the Populists had great hopes for electing a president four years later.

Those hopes were dashed by two factors: racial hatred and the presidential candidacy of a two-term Nebraska congressman named William Jennings Bryan. In 1892, for example, the Populist candidate for president, James B. Weaver, was harassed by hecklers and hooligans during a tour of the South. Night riders and other extralegal means were directed not just against African Americans, who tended to vote Republican, but Populists, who also threatened the rule of the Democratic Party in the region. Even at this late stage of industrial development, race was more important than class in determining the voting behavior of working-class Americans.

The rise of William Jennings Bryan proved to be a more serious threat to Populism because it gave voters an outlet to express their discontent inside the existing two-party system. Although he was a Democrat, Bryan's signature issue was the same as the Populists': "free silver." Free silver refers to efforts to base the amount of money in circulation not just on the amount of gold the government had, but on silver too. Financial interests opposed this plan because it was inflationary. More money in circulation would have meant that all money would have been worth less in real terms, but farmers supported free silver because they were almost all in debt. Free silver would mean that they could pay back those debts with money worth less than the money they borrowed. Bankers, of course, found that possibility horrifying.

Bryan's most famous moment during the 1896 campaign was all about this issue. In his "Cross of Gold" speech, speaking about big business, he argued that "We shall answer their demands for a gold standard by saying to them, you shall not press down upon the brow of labor this crown of thorns. You shall not crucify mankind upon a cross of gold."[14] Walter Lippmann, however, argued that what "Bryan and his people really hated from the bottom of their souls were the economic conditions which had upset the old life of the prairies, made new demands upon democracy, introduced specialization and science, destroyed village loyalties, frustrated private ambitions, and created the impersonal relationships of the modern world."[15] The gold standard was just a symbol of those changes, and those changes had been brought about by industrialization. Even if you did not work in a factory, the interests of industrial corporations and the rhythms of factory life reached into every corner of the United States.

It was Bryan's nomination for president that brought about the collapse of the Populist Party. To gain that nomination, Bryan had to defeat the conservative wing of the Democratic Party, the people who found the notion of free silver horrifying. Rather than split the vote by nominating another candidate who supported free silver, the Populists nominated Bryan too in 1896. As long as the Democrats supported the same key issue that the Populists did, voting for the major party made more sense. When the Democrats renominated Bryan in 1900 for what would be another losing candidacy, most farmers simply failed to return to the Populist fold. The party had done its best to reach out to labor to form a class-based coalition, but Populism never caught on in urban circles.

There were other reasons besides structural ones that explain the failure of the Populists to become a permanent political presence in America. In the South, Populists were race-baited, accused of showing a concern for African Americans that barely existed. This helped convince many poor white southerners to return to the Democratic fold despite their concerns about how the economic system had treated them. Democrats and Republicans alike did their best to prevent the Populists from establishing a permanent political presence in every region of the country through any means necessary (including illegal ones). It did not help that the most radical Populists were unwilling to support Bryan because he did not support the other planks in the Populist agenda, like the imposition of state-run railroads. Although the Populist Party finally folded in 1908, it had become irrelevant years before the turn of the twentieth century.

While short-lived, Populism pioneered an important critique of industrial capitalism that would be picked up by others in the future. Its calls for economic independence had an important effect upon the nation's economic agenda. Besides the unsuccessful efforts at implementing free silver, the Populists were strong opponents of monopolies. "The most distressing feature of this war of the Trusts," wrote Weaver, "is the fact that they control the articles which people consume in their daily life. It cuts off their accumulation and denies them the staff upon which they fain would lean in their old age."[16] Such rhetoric set the groundwork for Theodore Roosevelt's actions a decade later. The Populist Party's ideas also laid the groundwork for a much broader and much more successful reform effort that rose at about that same time.

The Progressive Movement

While generally unsuccessful, Populism firmly established the idea that government could be a countervailing force against the power of a business community swollen with economic power through the benefits of industrialization. Progressives like President Theodore Roosevelt imagined the role of government to embody complete neutrality between interests of all kinds. While this may seem like a mild goal today, compared to earlier years when big business essentially controlled government, it made a big difference in many people's lives. Industrialists were not the only danger in the post-Populist era. Radicals like the Socialist Eugene V. Debs were seen as a similar threat to the industrial order. Therefore, the reform movement that followed Populism and was designed to check the excesses of industrialization included many representatives of the middle- and upper-middle classes.

The Progressive Era lasted roughly from 1900 to 1914 (the year that World War I began). The Progressive movement active during that era encompassed many different kinds of reform. Nevertheless, one concern that united nearly every faction was an acute concern for the welfare of citizens. This was not something most government leaders supported during the years that laissez-faire and social Darwinism were being developed. It began with progressivism. Some factions of the movement were more interested in the economic welfare of citizens than others, but many aspects of progressivism (including ones that were not clearly economic in nature) were really efforts to fix problems created by industrialization. Perhaps the key central theme of progressivism was opposition to industrial organization like the great merger movement. Unorganized factions of society joined up to get protection against those that were already highly organized. Many small business owners, for example, became Progressives because they feared what they thought was unfair competition from their gigantic competitors.

The Pure Food and Drug Act of 1906 was one of the greatest Progressive success stories. It created what would become the Food and Drug Administration, which was supposed to safeguard the production of the foods Americans ate. While adulterated food and unsafe drugs had been a problem for decades, this problem had become considerably worse with the advent of industrialization because mechanization had increased the likelihood of unsafe food entering the stream of commerce. Large firms supported this kind of regulation because unscrupulous firms that used cheaper, improper ingredients could undersell their goods in the marketplace. With the government there to protect them, consumers were more likely to purchase products created in factories even if they did not understand exactly how (or with what) they were produced.

Prohibition supporters formed another faction within the Progressive movement. This cultural and religious reform grew out of the religious revivals of the early nineteenth century. Its eventual success in the early twentieth century came about, at least in part, as a result of the changes brought by industrialization. In 1890 the newspaper of the Women's Christian Temperance Union argued that "men and women, overworked, with a state of low vitality and innumerable difficulties to meet, naturally turn toward anything that will afford temporary relief . . . In the midst of misery, drinking is almost inevitable."[17] Some employers eventually joined the cause for financial reasons too. Workmen's compensation laws passed by states during the early years of the Progressive Era forced employers to contribute to a common fund to pay victims of workplace accidents. In response, employers threatened to fire heavy drinkers who seemed more prone to get hurt (which was ironic if you believe that the changes in workplace conditions created by industrialization likely drove at least some men to drink). Employers also contributed to Prohibition advocacy groups since the employers believed that all their workers would be more productive if they could no longer imbibe at all. The Volstead Act, implemented in 1920, was the enforcement mechanism for Prohibition. Its unexpected harshness signaled a break with Progressive Era politics and helped explain the failure of the entire experiment.

Another Progressive reform, the Mann Act of 1910, banned the transportation of women across state lines for immoral purposes. While the problem here was obviously moral, the underlying concern was commercial power run wild. In 1910 the superintendent of the Illinois Training School for Girls warned that "some 65,000 daughters of American homes and 15,000 alien girls are the prey each year of procurers in this traffic. . . . They are hunted, trapped in a thousand ways. . . . [and] sold—sold for less than hogs and held in white slavery worse than death."[18] These concerns were exaggerated. Investigators who interviewed 1,106 streetwalkers found only six who claimed white slavery was the cause of their entering that profession. In many cases prostitution was a solution for unemployment. Many women became prostitutes because they did not like their other economic opportunities. They could make more money as prostitutes than they could ever get working in a factory.

Finally, a federal income tax had been a Progressive priority since before the inception of the movement. The Supreme Court had invalidated such a tax as unconstitutional in 1895, but a new constitutional amendment made it legal again in 1914. When a weak income tax was first passed that same year, it was almost derailed by manufacturing interests that did not want the special tariffs on their goods repealed in order to keep government revenues essentially neutral. When preparing to enter World War I, Congress passed a new higher income tax in order to pay for preparedness initiatives. Most of the burden from that legislation fell upon the rich, the people who had been most likely to benefit from the industrial trend of previous decades. Since Progressives argued that paying more taxes was a sign of patriotism, this modest increase in government revenues was not at all controversial.

Historians have spilled lots of ink since the Progressive Era trying to define exactly what progressivism was and who participated in the movement. Obviously, not all factions in the Progressive movement were directly tied to industrialization and its effects. Nonetheless, an important advantage of looking at progressivism this way is that it demonstrates the relationship between progressivism and other important trends of this era, including the similarities between Progressives and Populists. Politics (except through the absence of adequate government regulation) did not play a significant role in most Americans' lives during the era of industrialization. Yet politics did do something to mitigate the effects of industrialization even when the will for government intervention was weak compared to what it would become later. Progressives set important precedents for the eventual founding of the American welfare state during the New Deal of the 1930s. Progressive reformers also encouraged private businesses to mitigate the negative effects of industrialization on a private basis. Some far-sighted capitalists had begun doing that with varied success before there even was a Progressive movement.

Notes

1. Walter Lippmann, *Drift and Mastery: An Attempt to Diagnose the Current Unrest* (New York: Mitchell Kennerly, 1914), 71.

2. Lippmann, 110.

3. Lippmann, 255.

4. James Bryce, *The American Commonwealth* (London: Macmillan & Co., 1889), 2:405.

5. In Richard Hofstadter, *The Age of Reform: From Bryan to F.D.R.* (New York: Vintage Books, 1955), 184.

6. Robert L. Heilbroner, *The Economic Transformation of America* (New York: Harcourt Brace Jovanovich, 1977), 113.

7. National Archives, "Transcript of Sherman Antitrust Act (1890)," Our Documents, www.ourdocuments.gov/doc.php?flash=true&doc=51&page=transcript.

8. Heilbroner, 112.

9. In Gabriel Kolko, *The Triumph of Conservatism: A Reinterpretation of American History, 1900–1916* (New York: Free Press, 1963), 68.

10. *Northern Securities Co. v. United States*, 193 U.S. 197 (1904).

11. Halvor Harris to Ignatius Donnelly, January 29, 1891, in *The Populist Mind*, ed. Norman Pollack (Indianapolis: Bobbs Merrill, 1967), 33–34.

12. Mary Elizabeth Lease, "Wall Street Owns the Country," in *Voices of a People's History of the United States*, ed. Howard Zinn and Anthony Arnove (New York: Seven Stories Press, 2004), 226.

13. In Charles Postel, *The Populist Vision* (New York: Oxford University Press, 2007), 158–159.

14. William Jennings Bryan, "Mr. Bryan's Speech at the Chicago Convention," *Review of Reviews* 14 (August 1896): 176.

15. Lippmann, 130.

16. In Michael Kazin, *The Populist Persuasion: An American History* (New York: Basic Books, 1995), 41.

17. In Nell Irvin Painter, *Standing at Armageddon: The United States, 1877–1919* (New York: W.W. Norton, 1987), 63.

18. In James R. Petersen, *The Century of Sex: Playboy's History of the Sexual Revolution, 1900–1999* (New York: Grove Press, 1999), 22–23.

Reform

Q. *Could the harmful effects of industrialization on people be mitigated by the private sector?*

In 1872 the photographer Eadweard Muybridge began a series of experiments at the behest of Leland Stanford, one of the organizers of the Central Pacific Railroad. Stanford wanted to answer the question whether his trotting racehorse, Occident, ever had all its legs off the ground at the same time while moving. The East Coast racing establishment thought "yes"; Stanford and his West Coast friends thought the opposite. Muybridge had been interested in what was known as "instantaneous photography" in order to illustrate motion for some time. Here was a chance to try out this new technology in practice. Muybridge used twelve cameras laid out along the animal's path, with electronically controlled shutters to photograph the horse's movements in sequence. Muybridge's single image of Occident with all four legs off the ground illustrated the horse's position for about a five-hundredth of a second. When released to the general public for the first time in 1878, that single image disproved hundreds of years of artists' depictions of moving horses, but it was also a triumph of industrialization. Modern inventions had shown that movement in nature could be broken down into pieces and studied, the same way that industrialists divided labor.

Muybridge was hailed by both artists and scientists for his work with Stanford. His experiments changed how people thought not only about horses, but about motion in general. Muybridge took these kinds of studies to audiences around the world using another kind of technology, the "magic lantern" slideshow, to simulate the subjects of his pictures in motion. "Nothing was wanting," reported the *San Francisco Daily Call* about one of Muybridge's presentations that focused upon the movement of horses, "but the clatter of hoofs upon the turf and the occasional breath of steam from the nostrils, to make the spectator believe that he had before him genuine flesh-and-blood steeds."[1] These techniques were

Eadweard Muybridge made his reputation as an artist and a scientist photographing and depicting horses in motion.

an obvious precursor of Edison's motion pictures, not to mention the modern PowerPoint program. At these talks, Muybridge would entertain his audiences not just with the pictures themselves, but by explaining how a better understanding of motion could improve art, athletics, and especially engineering. Studying the movement of workers, for instance, would make it possible for them to learn how to make those movements in such a way that they would do less damage to the worker's health.

In 1884 Muybridge's fame as a scientist brought him to the University of Pennsylvania in Philadelphia. He was supposed to photograph medical patients who walked strangely so that medical students could study their deformity. Instead, Muybridge spent much of his time photographing college athletes in motion. Often depicted naked—like the ancient Greek statues that were popular during this era—these figures were designed to inspire people to avoid neurasthenia, the kind of "American nervousness" that George Beard had defined just a few years before. By moving as smoothly and efficiently as possible, people would not expend the supposed "nervous energy" that powered them through their daily lives on wasted actions. The treatment of the subjects in the photographs—

scientific, clinical, outwardly asexual—suggests that Muybridge intended to treat the human body like a machine. Other sequences that Muybridge photographed at the university show ordinary people doing ordinary things such as jumping, sweeping, or dancing. Often these subjects were also depicted completely naked.

These montages may have been designed to illustrate the possible treatments for neurasthenia. One of his colleagues at the university was the psychologist Silas Weir Mitchell, who would go on to invent the "rest cure" for depressed women who he believed needed to avoid the stimulation of modern life. (This was precisely the vicious kind of mental "treatment" that would inspire Charlotte Perkins Gilman to write the story "The Yellow Wallpaper.") If Muybridge's work in Philadelphia really was designed to combat neurasthenia, it carried great irony. Photographers were not considered artists during the 1880s. Instead, the art establishment still saw them as machine operators. Muybridge's work, then, used machines to help fix the ill effects of other machines.

That may seem strange, but by this date business had been using science to fix problems of all kinds since industrialization had begun. Applied science referred to the practice of studying the world in order to solve problems rather than to make money. Systematic invention, a technique developed by Thomas Edison, meant utilizing one's energy to solve a particular problem with great commercial potential. Edison had been perturbed by the failure of his first invention, a machine that counted votes in legislatures, to find a market. Even something as technologically innovative as the phonograph player had little market when it was developed. (Edison thought it would be used for dictation.) The light bulb, however, negated the ill effects of dirty kerosene lighting. Everything Edison invented in order to generate and transport electricity was designed to solve the problem of bringing electricity to consumers so that they could run those light bulbs and other electrical appliances.

Technology had more trouble solving the problems of human beings than it did the problems of other machines. People are inherently complicated. Satisfying their needs and catering to their wants can never be an exact science. Therefore, most of the efforts to reform industrialization dealt primarily with its effects upon workers in one way or another. As machines became more efficient and reliable during the era of industrialization, the effects of those changes on workers grew steadily worse. Splitting the proceeds of industrialization evenly between labor and management was off the table in a capitalist economy;

therefore employers tested various ways to improve the productivity of both people and machines, seeing just how much change workers were willing to accept.

"The problem of increasing the production per man was one which could not be solved by speeding up machinery and by improving technical processes," wrote the economist Paul Douglas in 1919. "American industry soon found that the proper handling of labor was necessary in order to realize maximum efficiency."[2] But what was the proper handling of labor? Countless reformers suggested many different policies designed to keep industrial workers happy and productive. Political reformers got laws passed that created minimum wages and limited the length of the working day in order to make the conditions that working-class people faced a little less dire. Employers themselves developed a new kind of welfare that originated from them rather than the state in order to make their employees' lives more content. Other reformers created social uplift programs that taught immigrant workers the value of hard work and the kinds of living habits that made the workers more acceptable to their native-born employers and colleagues on the job. While these experiments sometimes met with short-term success, greed often doomed them to failure in the long run.

Taylorism

Like Muybridge, Frederick Winslow Taylor was concerned with the nature of motion, but he wanted to use that knowledge in the service of capitalism. Taylor, part of a well-to-do Philadelphia family, began the systematic study of work as a lecturer and private consultant at eastern Pennsylvania steel companies in the 1880s and 1890s. Ironically, he was not particularly successful at increasing production at those steel mills, but he still managed to become famous because he expressed his ideas in a way that captured the essence of the era. Taylor's ideas are embodied in his book *The Principles of Scientific Management*, first published in 1911.

At the beginning of the book, Taylor emphasizes the importance of conserving natural resources, citing President Theodore Roosevelt's efforts to preserve virgin forests. But the resource that Taylor wanted to conserve was the strength of workers, who by his estimate too often wasted that strength by moving in an inefficient manner on the job. Ending that waste of motion, Taylor thought, would obviously benefit

Frederick Winslow Taylor's idea of scientific management has affected the way that employers of all kinds utilize their labor even today.

management, but also it would create what he called "first-class men," efficient employees who would then be able to keep more of the benefits of that efficiency for themselves, thereby mitigating the negative effects of industrialization on those workers. While Taylor's categories for workers were rife with ethnic stereotypes, to employers of all kinds this seemed like real science.

Scientific management has become so identified with Taylor that it is often called Taylorism. In order to implement his principles, Taylor would look at how a particular set of workers did their job and then break up the process into its component parts. To do this, he timed workers with stopwatches. Other scientific management enthusiasts would film workers so as to see and understand every motion they made. From this information Taylor would determine the one best way to do that job, often breaking it up into smaller tasks so that the workers would do the same thing over and over again.

In order to get employees to work harder, Taylor recommended that employers implement piece rates: payment by output rather than by job. To determine where the piece rate should be set, he made an arbitrary decision as to how fast a normal worker should be going and then set the piece rate to reflect that. The advantage of this system was that if the employees met this standard, employers could lower the piece rate and get workers working even harder to reach the same rate. This is known as the speedup. Workers hate it because it makes them work harder without additional reward. It also divides them from each other, when they might have worked together to keep operations moving at a more manageable speed. Managers referred to that practice as soldiering, and they considered it indefensible, a sign that workers were in truth lazy and undeserving.

The speedup may be a corruption of Taylorism, but it was the essence of capitalism. Managers wanted absolute control over the production process so that they could reap most of the benefits of it for themselves. As Taylor explained, "The managers assume . . . the burden of gathering together all of the traditional knowledge which in the past has been possessed by the workmen, then of classifying, tabulating, and reducing this knowledge to laws, rules and formulas."[3] The second reason to adopt the process was to take knowledge away from the workers and give it to employers. Employers could then use that knowledge in order to rationalize the production process, making it more efficient. When workers had the knowledge, they often used it to slow down production. Taylor hated that. On the other hand, many skilled workers hated scientific management because it made their jobs less interesting and more strenuous and it often led to lower pay. More importantly, if employers could replace a worker with many responsibilities by more workers with fewer responsibilities, it made skilled workers expendable.

The symbol of Taylorism and the focal point of resistance to its principles was his stopwatch. The best-known example of the revolt against Taylorism was at the Watertown Arsenal in Massachusetts. Scientific management was gradually introduced there beginning in 1909, two years before the publication of Taylor's book. The skilled iron molders there hated the system when it was adopted in the foundry department in 1911. "The very unsatisfactory conditions which have prevailed in the foundry among the molders for the past week or more reached an acute stage this afternoon when a man was seen to use a stop watch on one of the molders," they all wrote in a letter to the commander of the arsenal. "This we believe to be the limit of our endurance. It is humiliating to us, who have always tried to give to the Government the best that was in us. This method was un-American in principal, and we most respectfully request that you have it discontinued at once."[4] Before the petition was even handed in, one employee was fired for resisting being timed. All the molders in the foundry walked out at once without the authorization of their union. The Taylor system thus actually strengthened union organization in this instance because everybody hated it so much and admired the union for taking a strong stand against it. Nevertheless, the molders were all back at work within a week and the time studies disappeared.

In 1915, after long congressional hearings, Congress banned the introduction of the Taylor system at all government facilities. Taylor defended his system at the hearings for the bill, and then died shortly afterward. After this conflict, future scientific managers would concentrate on obtaining employee consent for these changes, but that does not mean managers actually followed their advice. Once employers knew they could get their labor force to work at an accelerated pace, they could not resist the temptation to cut incentive pay so that workers had to labor even harder to earn the same amount in total compensation. These speedups in many industries negated whatever positive impact that Taylor's reforms had. Despite such abuse of Taylor's system, his ideas remain influential to the present day.

Fordism

Like Taylor, Henry Ford believed in the value of efficiency. However, he was not just interested in the efficiency of labor. He reorganized his factories in such a way to maximize production and to share the benefits of that production with his workers. "Ford's success . . . exhibits in higher degree than most persons would have thought possible the seemingly contradictory requirements of true efficiency," explained a book written with Ford's cooperation in 1915. The hallmarks of efficiency that Ford had supposedly achieved were a "constant increase of quality, great increase of pay to the workers, repeated reductions in cost to the consumer," and "an absolutely incredible enlargement of output reaching something like one hundred fold in less than ten years," which resulted in "an enormous profit to the manufacturer."[5] Ford, it seemed, had achieved the impossible: industrialization that benefited labor, management, and consumers alike. This was the essence of Fordism, perhaps the most far-reaching set of reforms to industrialization since the process had begun over a century earlier.

Ford's success was only possible because he—with a lot of help from his many engineers—arranged the company's factories in order to achieve

The principle behind the Ford Motor Company's assembly line was to bring the parts of the car to the workers rather than make the workers move to where the parts of the car were. *(Courtesy of the Library of Congress)*

maximum throughput. While sometimes defined as the productivity of a factory, throughput is actually a measure of the speed and volume of the flow of goods through the production process. The arrangement of a factory had an enormous effect on throughput. Starting in the 1880s, inventors developed new machinery like conveyors and rollers, which made production through a continuous process possible. Ford placed his machines as close together as possible. This saved employees from making wasted movements.

Ford's interest in the efficiency of production culminated in the development of the assembly line between 1913 and 1914. Ford could not design this process simply by having raw materials dropped at one end of the plant and cars driven out the other. He experimented with creating different sections of the automobile on the assembly line. The big leap in speed and production came when the company started using the assembly line to move chassis through the system. When that central assembly began operating, the time it took to assemble a chassis dropped from twelve hours and twenty-eight minutes to one hour and thirty-three minutes. The lines for assembling parts were gradually linked to this central line by conveyors to create a mostly seamless operation.

Only the longest conveyors then known could make this arrangement possible for something as complicated as an automobile. Ford's giant River Rouge factory complex near Detroit, finished in 1928, included a car frame and assembly plant, a tire-making plant, a metal stamping plant, an engine casting plant, a transmission plant, a radiator plant, a tool and die plant, and a gigantic power plant so that all the parts needed for an automobile would be close at hand. Ford saw that wasted motion hurt efficiency so he made sure that all the machines were packed tightly together to increase throughput even more. At its peak during the 1930s, the factory produced one new Ford every forty-nine seconds. Only a company with the ability to manage a mass distribution system like Ford could ever hope to sell so many cars.

The fundamental innovation of the assembly line was to bring the product to the workers rather than workers to the product. Every piece that went into that car moved, not by human labor but by mechanical conveyance. "We now have two general principles in all operation," wrote Ford in his autobiography, "that a man shall never have to take more than one step, if possibly it can be avoided, and that no man need ever stoop over."[6] This saved effort and made it possible to greatly increase the speed of production. Over time, Ford's assembly line got successively longer. More labor hours were saved and output skyrocketed as a result. Recognizing the revolutionary nature of this success, Ford and his engineers correctly suggested that these principles could be applied to the manufacture of just about anything. But what were the costs of this increase in production?

The assembly line was the natural result of a business geared toward shortening the time of assembly as much as possible. It also kept everyone on the line working at the same speed, which meant that soldiering effort was absolutely impossible. Ford and his engineers had to conduct many experiments to set the speed of the line at the ideal rate. "The idea is that a man must not be hurried in his work," explained Ford later; "he must have every second necessary but not a single unnecessary second."[7] To Ford, this was a compromise since it balanced the abilities of the workers against the interests of production. Nevertheless, only the most patient of people could work under these conditions, for this was very difficult work. "The chain system you have is a slavedriver!" wrote the anonymous wife of a Ford worker in a letter to the boss. "My God!, Mr. Ford. My husband has come home & thrown himself down and won't eat his supper—so done out! Can't it be remedied?"[8] Besides the extra effort, another cause of turnover at Ford was boredom. An employee on the assembly line was tasked with doing the same thing all day. This was the division of labor carried to the fullest extent possible. In 1913, while experiments with the assembly line were not even finished, Ford had to hire 963 men in order to find 100 who were willing to work under such conditions.

These problems explain why Henry Ford introduced the five-dollar day in 1914, which more than doubled wages for most of his workers. That wage, unprecedented at that time, brought accusations from other employers that Ford was a traitor to his class. Of course, Ford had a good business reason for paying so much, even if this was not really a remedy for the situation that the assembly line created. It was a reward to workers for toiling under the difficult conditions that the assembly line created. For most workers a high wage with a lot of work to do was usually better than a low wage, but Ford did not give five dollars per day to just anyone. At first the company claimed that 90 percent of its workforce would get the five-dollar day, but then the firm tightened its standards. In order to be eligible for this wage, workers had to be married or have dependents at home. Unmarried men and women did not get this perk. Over time, employees had to be able to demonstrate that they did not drink alcohol, saved a portion of their paycheck, and had good moral character in order to be eligible for the five-dollar day. As thousands of workers migrated to Detroit in the hope of getting Ford's extraordinary wage, the company insisted that workers had to reside in Detroit for six months prior to becoming eligible. By the end of 1914, the company decided that much of its workforce was ineligible for such aid. Despite such holes, Ford management pointed to the five-dollar day more often than it did its own industrial technology in order to explain its high productivity.

The enforcement arm for such policies was Ford's Sociological Department, which had begun in 1912, but became a crucial part of Ford's policies only after the five-dollar day began. It enforced these policies by employing a battalion of investigators to visit their employees' homes. Investigators made suggestions to improve the lives of employees, but those who could not live up to Ford's principles risked being terminated. Ironically, Ford's Sociological Department came into being because studies at the time showed that happy workers were more productive. Therefore, other employers created a whole bevy of other programs designed to mitigate the adverse effects of industrialization and keep workers happy.

Welfare Capitalism

In 1883 George Pullman established a new factory to make railroad cars just south of Chicago. The Pullman Palace Car was a luxury passenger car for America's rapidly expanding railroads. Surrounding the factory, Pullman built the first model industrial town in America. It had a hotel, a restaurant, a saloon, a post office, a bank, and a multidenominational church where a different religious group held services at different hours every Sunday. The entire town, including the homes of the workers who built Pullman cars, was owned by the Pullman Palace Car Company. Pullman undertook this endeavor in order to make capitalism more humane. At the same time, he believed that these efforts would impress workers enough that they would be less likely to join unions and/or strike for higher pay. Pullman also banned alcohol consumption within city limits, believing, as many employers did, that sober workers were more productive.

After the turn of the twentieth century, this kind of paternalism would get a name: "welfare work." A 1923 book devoted entirely to the subject of welfare work defined it as any effort "to establish and maintain certain standards in respect to hours, wages, working and living conditions of his employees which are neither required by law nor by the conditions of the market."[9] Yet such a definition is still excessively broad. Welfare capitalism encompassed an enormous number of endeavors, so many that even the practitioners of this idea were not entirely certain what it entailed. There were, indeed, few limitations as to what constituted welfare capitalism. Different kinds of welfare capitalism included company baseball teams, pensions, gardens for employees, practical nurses to teach immigrant wives hygiene and housekeeping, company hospitals, swimming pools, marching bands, and many other efforts designed to make working in an industrialized setting easier.

Employers have always provided goods or services for their employees that were not required by law or the market. Only in the late nineteenth century was an increase in such opportunities touted as an answer to the "labor question." Spurred on by Progressive Era reform groups, welfare capitalism exploded onto the American economic scene around the turn of the century. National Cash Register, International Harvester, General Electric, H.J. Heinz, and U.S. Steel were just a few of the large American corporations that created elaborate welfare programs between 1890 and 1910. About 1920 welfare capitalism expanded into nearly every sector of the American economy.

Housing was a particularly important kind of welfare capitalism because every employee needed somewhere to live. Employers have always had to provide housing for employees in remote areas, but the advent of welfare capitalism brought on the first company towns, where most of the real estate was owned by the employer; Pullman, Illinois, is one of the best known examples. Most of the housing invariably went to skilled workers whom companies would have had trouble replacing. Unskilled workers either had to fend for themselves or live in terrible conditions.

Another form of welfare capitalism was profit sharing. The most popular form of profit sharing was the stock ownership plan. Employers would take a little bit out of workers' paychecks each month and put it away to pay for stock they had already given to the workers. This was supposed to put the workers on the same side as the employers: all would now be working together for their own financial good. As one company chair insisted, stock ownership "makes the wage earner an actual partner . . . a real capitalist. . . . They have a keen desire to see the institutions of this country protected as those who have greater riches, and they may be relied upon to lend their influence and their votes in favor of the protection of property and person."[10] Key large companies like U.S. Steel and International Harvester started stock subscription programs before World War I, and they were perceived to be so successful that nearly 400 different companies had stock ownership programs in 1927.

One problem with stock ownership was that few workers could afford to participate in such programs. During the 1920s more workers could afford stock ownership. On the downside, they were susceptible to the risks of stock ownership, as the October 1929 market crash made abundantly clear. During the Depression, when some workers could not afford to eat, few could afford stock. All these programs were quietly discontinued. Another problem with these bonus plans was that they were obvious attempts at social control. Failure to do what management wanted could cause the workers' benefits to be terminated, so many employees who could afford to participate in such programs chose not to do so.

In the decades before Social Security, many companies established private pension plans that would take care of employees in old age. Faithful service would be faithfully rewarded. The problem with these programs was that few employees, especially unskilled employees, expected to stay with one employer for their whole careers. Many knew they would be let go for long stretches as demand for the product they produced ebbed and flowed. Another problem was that as more and more employees qualified for the pension, employers tended to tighten eligibility requirements, making the retirement age older and the qualifying years longer, because they did not want their pensions to drain their treasuries. This meant that the percentage of pensioners to total employees was often kept at a low level. The failure of private pensions to take care of this problem is one reason that a sizable number of employers supported Social Security in 1935. We cannot do it, the companies essentially argued, so let the government do it.

Employers were interested in welfare capitalism for reasons of paternalism. Despite a near universal belief in the supremacy of the profit motive, many employers felt they owed it to their workers to treat them right. They considered it their responsibility as successful business owners to help those who were less successful to uplift themselves. Some employers equated goodness and profit, but many business owners denied profit had anything to do with it. Unfortunately, this kind of paternalism often created extraordinary resentment. As one of Pullman's workers complained, "We are born in a Pullman house, fed from the Pullman shop, taught in the Pullman school, catechized in the Pullman church, and when we die, we shall be buried in the Pullman cemetery and go to the Pullman Hell."[11] Such sentiments, coupled with Pullman's refusal to maintain his largesse during the Panic of 1893, led to the infamous Pullman Strike of 1894.

The other reason for implementing welfare capitalist policies was public relations. Doing right by the employees led to good press, which in turn improved the company's public image. Indeed, many firms that treated their employees well would brag about it in order to improve their image. Many welfare capitalist firms were antiunion, so when they got bogged down in strikes they could cite welfare capitalism as a reason why unions were not necessary, which in the end undercut the power of industrial reform. In light of the overwhelming profits that industrialization brought America's largest businesses, the American power structure would only let reform go so far. The same remains true today.

Notes

1. In Rebecca Solnit, *River of Shadows: Eadweard Muybridge and the Technological Wild West* (New York: Penguin, 2004), 203.

2. Paul H. Douglas, "Plant Administration of Labor," *Journal of Political Economy* 27 (July 1919): 545–546.

3. Frederick Winslow Taylor, *The Principles of Scientific Management* (New York: Harper & Brothers, 1911), 36.

4. In Robert Kanigel, *The One Best Way: Frederick Winslow Taylor and the Enigma of Efficiency* (New York: Viking, 1997), 452–453.

5. Horace Lucien Arnold and Fay Leone Faurote, *Ford Methods and the Ford Shops* (New York: Engineering Magazine Company, 1915), iii.

6. Henry Ford, *My Life and Work* (Garden City, NY: Doubleday, Page & Co., 1923), 80.

7. Ford, 82.

8. In David A. Hounshell, *From the American System to Mass Production, 1800–1932* (Baltimore: Johns Hopkins University Press, 1984), 259.

9. In Jonathan Rees, *Managing the Mills: Labor Policy in the American Steel Industry During the Nonunion Era* (Lanham, MD: University Press of America, 2004), 105.

10. In Lizabeth Cohen, *Making a New Deal: Industrial Workers in Chicago, 1919–1939* (New York: Cambridge University Press, 2008), 175.

11. In Philip Dray, *There Is Power in a Union: The Epic Story of Labor in America* (New York: Doubleday, 2010), 191.

Epilogue

Q: *Were the benefits of industrialization worth the costs?*

The Corliss Engine was the centerpiece of the Machinery Hall at the 1876 Centennial Exposition in Philadelphia. Its designer, George Corliss, had first established his reputation by improving steam engines during the late 1840s. The large engine he built for the Expositon powered every other machine in the hall. The Corliss Engine was both powerful (many reporters incorrectly claimed it was the most powerful engine ever built) and aesthetically impressive. One of the catalogues describing the exhibit called it "that wonder of the modern era, that thing which puts the breath of life . . . to be a creation. . . . There it stands, holding its place among as a veritable king of machinery, so powerful and yet so gentle . . . without whose labor our efforts would be small indeed; the breathing pulse, the soul of the machinery exhibit."[1] This kind of reaction was so common that the engine became the best-known attraction at the entire fair. It makes sense that a large machine that ran every other machine in the hall would attract so much attention, as such machines represented the essence of the age.

When the historian and memoirist Henry Adams saw the successor to the Corliss Engine, an electric generator (or dynamo) up close for the first time at the Paris Exposition of 1900, he was much more ambivalent about progress. "To him," Adams wrote (in the third person), "the dynamo itself was but an ingenious channel for conveying somewhere the heat latent in a few tons of poor coal hidden in a dirty engine-house carefully kept out of sight, but to Adams the dynamo became a symbol of infinity." In less than a quarter century, the source of power for machinery had moved from the center of the stage to offstage as far as visitors were concerned. It was no longer that big a deal. Yet Adams's reaction to the dynamo grew stronger as he toured the exposition hall full of machines that the generator powered: "He began to feel the forty-foot dynamos as a moral force, much as the early Christians felt the Cross. The planet itself

The Corliss Engine not only powered all the exhibits in the machinery hall at the Philadelphia Centennial Exposition of 1876, it was also a major attraction because it represented the power of industrialization. *(Courtesy of the Library of Congress)*

seemed less impressive, in its old-fashioned, deliberate, annual or daily revolution, than this huge wheel. . . . Before the end, one began to pray to it."[2] While obviously conservative in the cultural sense of that word, Adams was not antitechnology. He was impressed by the genius it took to harness so much energy for man's benefit, but it scared him when he tried to put the achievements of this feat into a broader perspective.

Woodrow Wilson, in his 1913 inaugural address, was less ambivalent about industrialization than Adams. Nevertheless, as was befitting the first Progressive Democratic president, he was willing to talk about its costs and benefits:

"We have been proud of our industrial achievements, but we have not hitherto stopped thoughtfully enough to count the human cost, the cost of lives snuffed out, of energies overtaxed and broken, the fearful physical and spiritual cost to the men and women and children upon whom the dead weight and burden of it all has fallen pitilessly the years through. The groans and agony of it all had not yet reached our ears, the solemn, moving undertone of our life, coming up out of the mines and factories, and out of every home where the struggle had its intimate and familiar seat.[3]

By now historians have made sure that the groans and agony caused by industrialization have been heard by succeeding generations, but the ability to read both sides of the story does not answer the crucial question whether the many benefits of industrialization were worth its many costs.

How you saw industrialization depends to a great extent upon the economic position from which you experienced it. The financial beneficiaries of this process obviously looked upon it favorably, but there were many losers too. "I am in alarm lest my all should be swept away," wrote a failed New Orleans salesman to the oil baron John D. Rockefeller in 1891, appealing for financial assistance. "I will hold my grip however the best I can & feel I will come out all right yet, especially if someone would step up & give me a little boost & encouragement."[4] Even someone as successful as the writer Mark Twain found himself in severe financial trouble after investing a substantial amount of money into a typesetting machine that never worked well. He turned his finances over to one of the founders of Rockefeller's Standard Oil in order to escape bankruptcy. The greatest victims of industrialization, though, were ordinary factory workers. They received little of the financial benefit of this process yet bore the brunt of its effects. As a new revolution changes the nature of the American economy today, the differing impact of such significant changes remains as true as ever.

Yesterday and Today

While it has become cliché to speak about the effects of the Internet on work—the so-called communications revolution—there is no doubt that methods of production, particularly knowledge production, have changed drastically in recent years in both good and bad ways. The *New York Times* columnist Tom Friedman argued as early as 2005 that the effect of global computer communication was to make the world flat. This, in turn, meant that "we are now connecting all the knowledge centers on the planet together into a single global network, which—if politics and terrorism do not get in the way—could usher in an amazing era of prosperity and innovation."[5] Certainly greater access to information makes many things possible that would not have happened otherwise (including the writing this book).

This development also has significant costs. In the same way that workers during the era of industrialization were replaced by machines, workers today are being displaced through changes brought about by computers and the global information network that they run. Bank tellers are replaced by ATMs. Newspaper reporters are replaced by new online-only sources for current news and the public's general preference to read other distractions available online. The futurist Jeremy Rifkin saw the problem with technology way back in 1995, before many Americans had ever heard of the Internet. "In the past," he wrote, "when new technologies have replaced workers in a given sector, new sectors have always emerged to absorb the displaced laborers. Today, all three of the traditional sectors of the economy—agriculture, manufacturing, and service—are experiencing technological displacement, forcing millions onto the unemployment rolls."[6] Such changes could be terribly jarring all by themselves, but the technology sector was growing then and is still growing now. Unfortunately, as Rifkin noted, that sector could not possibly absorb all the workers from other sectors that technology could displace. The Great Recession of 2008, followed by the "jobless recovery" of later years, only demonstrates the extent of Rifkin's foresight.

Today new immigrants from both hemispheres fill the lowest jobs on the American economic ladder. Their motivations are the same as those of immigrants during the era of industrialization. The motivations of immigration restriction proponents continue along the economic and racist lines of their forerunners. What has changed in this increasingly global economy is that it is now possible for foreign workers to compete against the native-born American worker without ever entering the United States. Cheap transportation and low tariffs around the globe make it possible for products manufactured all over the world to be sold anywhere else at a considerable profit. As a result, the industrialization that changed America a hundred years ago is repeating itself in new countries, and American workers experience the same kinds of economic pressures as a result.

Like Friedman, many people during the late nineteenth century saw tremendous potential in a technological future. For example, the economist Carroll Wright, then chief of the Massachusetts Bureau of Labor

Statistics, told the American Social Science Association in 1882 that machinery "has brought with it new phases of civilization, for while it means the factory system in one sense, it is the type and representative of the civilization of this period, because it embodies, so far as mechanics are concerned, the concentrated, clearly wrought out thought of the age. While books represent thought, machinery is the embodiment of thought."[7] Life itself might have seemed chaotic to most people, but factories were becoming more modern, more rational, and, of course, more profitable as a result of changes in technology. But what about the people who did not share equally in such benefits?

Like Rifkin, the most severe critics of industrialization focused upon its effects on labor as its greatest evil. But unlike the vague American nervousness that George Beard described, the effects of factory work upon the workers themselves were clearly visible. For example, when the writer Hamlin Garland visited Andrew Carnegie's Homestead works, his guide told him that "the long hours, the strain, the sudden change of temperature use a man up. He quits before he gets fifty. I can see lots of fellows here who are failing." Another worker Garland talked to was more abstract. "You start in to be man," he said, "but you become more and more a machine and pleasures are few and far between. It's like any severe labor, it drags you down mentally and morally, just as it does physically."[8] Material goods did not adequately compensate workers for this kind of damage. They worked because they had to in order to survive. Once they could no longer work, they struggled to endure.

As the effects of accelerated industrialization grew more visible with age, it became easier to observe many such victims of industrialization visible across many different industries. "It was long before we came to realize that in the depths of our steamships were those who fed the fires with their lives," wrote the author William Dean Howells, "and that our mines from which we dug our wealth were the graves of those who had died to the free light and air, without finding the rest of death. We did not see that the machines for labor saving were monsters that devoured women and children, and wasted men at the bidding of the power which no man must touch."[9] People who did not work in factories, of course, did not see the machines at all. They only saw the products that the factories produced, and therefore it was easy for them to take technology for granted.

What is ironic here is that mechanization might have allowed workers to work better if it were not for the way that employers drove people in an endless quest for profit. Too many manufacturers treated their employees like machines, and their employees responded badly to such treatment if they had the nerve to respond at all. It was not the process that liberated people but the goods that industrialization produced. Cheaper household products—everything from clothing to meat, candles to furniture—meant more people could enjoy greater material wealth. Perhaps more importantly, they no longer had to utilize their own labor to produce these goods for household consumption. Women's work in particular became much easier because of the products created through industrialization. Cheaper stuff helped everybody, rich and poor, unless you had to make a living manufacturing those products.

The Shock of the New

New technology was all around Americans during the late nineteenth and early twentieth centuries. It changed how they traveled, what they wore on their backs, and even what they ate. Nevertheless, the effects of this technology were quickly forgotten by most of its beneficiaries. As Henry Adams's brother Charles Francis explained about his life's work, railroads, "Whatever constantly enters into the daily life soon becomes an unnoticed part of it, so much a part of our everyday acts and thoughts that they have become familiar."[10] Meatpacking firms used to give tours through the Chicago stockyards during the era of industrialization to show off its wonders. "They make a great feature of showing strangers through the packing-plants," reported the writer and social activist Upton Sinclair in his well-researched novel, *The Jungle*, "for it is a good advertisement."[11] Today, in order to film inside most meatpacking plants you have to smuggle in a secret camera. Meatpackers do not want the shock of the old to become new again.

The history of late American industrialization suggests that people only notice the impact of this process when it is relatively new. Over time, the machines fade into the background, particularly those machines that most people have never seen. It takes fresh eyes to appreciate the extraordinary accomplishments of this era. "It was not until I had seen the water-works at Chicago that I realised the wonders of machinery," wrote the English writer Oscar Wilde after an American tour during the 1890s; "the rise and fall of the steel rods, the symmetrical motion of great wheels is the most beautifully rhythmic thing I have ever seen." But Wilde also saw the bad in such accomplishments: "One is impressed in America, but not favourably impressed, by the inordinate size of everything. The country seems to try to bully one into a belief in its power by its impressive bigness."[12] Perhaps intimidation was part of the reason that most Chicagoans undoubtedly forgot how much machinery was required in order to bring water to their taps.

The effects of American industrialization were readily apparent in Wilde's home country, the place where industrialization had begun during the late eighteenth century. "Ten years ago England was easily first in the iron, shipping, cotton and coal industries," wrote an alarmed British observer in 1901. "We took from America raw food products in considerable quantities, but America was our greatest customer for manufactured goods. Now the situation is changed. America has already far outstripped us in iron and steel-making, it is making great gaps in our shipping business, it is seriously competing with us in cotton and is planning to take from us our export coal trade." In fact, the relationship between America and Great Britain had started to resemble the colonial relationship it once was but with the roles reversed. "Where not long since America was our largest customer," this observer continued, "we are now the biggest and most profitable buyers from America. The United States Government reports declare that England takes seventy-nine per cent, of their products sent to Europe, and sixty per cent, of all the products which the American farmer sends abroad."[13] That this particular book got published in the United States as well as England suggests that Americans enjoyed having their newfound power acknowledged.

This kind of dominance was no accident. While America was not a colonial power in the same sense that its older European rivals were, America did seek a role in the world in large part to ensure that there would always be markets for its industrial surplus. "We must have new markets," argued the expansionist Senator Henry Cabot Lodge, "unless we would be visited by declines in wages and by great industrial disturbances of which signs have not been lacking."[14] Not every advocate of overseas economic expansion was quite as utilitarian as Lodge. For example, President Wilson told an audience of salesmen in 1916 to "go out and sell goods that will make the world more comfortable and happy, and convert them to the principles of America."[15] The products of factories, in other words, were mighty advertisements for democracy and the advantages of the American way of life. Such thinking would become increasingly commonplace as America entered the Cold War.

Today the roles have begun to reverse again—not the roles between America and Europe but the relationship between America and places like China, which we used to see as nothing more than a market for our goods. Now we are a market for goods produced there, albeit goods often produced under the auspices of Western corporations. This has given rise to a new phenomenon: deindustrialization. One-time powerhouse industrial communities like Flint, Michigan, and Pittsburgh, Pennsylvania, have shed jobs or transformed entirely in response to foreign competition. But the collapse of American industry has only been possible because of industrialization in other countries. Our past is their present. In this way, the question of whether the benefits of industrialization are worth the costs remains relevant today.

Notes

1. In John F. Kasson, *Civilizing the Machine: Technology and Republican Values in America, 1776–1900* (New York: Hill & Wang, 1999), 164.

2. Henry Adams, *The Education of Henry Adams: An Autobiography* (Boston: Houghton Mifflin, 1918), 380.

3. In Jack Beatty, *Age of Betrayal: The Triumph of Money in America, 1865–1900* (New York: Alfred A. Knopf, 2007), 390–391.

4. In Scott A. Sandage, *Born Losers: A History of Failure in America* (Cambridge, MA: Harvard University Press, 2005), 250.

5. Thomas L. Friedman, *The World Is Flat: A Brief History of the Twenty-First Century* (New York: Farrar, Straus and Giroux, 2005), 8.

6. Jeremy Rifkin, *The End of Work: The Decline of the Global Labor Force and the Dawn of the Post-Market Era* (New York: G.P. Putnam's Sons, 1995), xvi.

7. Carroll D. Wright, "The Factory System As an Element of Civilization," *Journal of Social Science* 16 (December 1882): 119.

8. Hamlin Garland, "Homestead and Its Perilous Trades," *McClure's Magazine* 3 (June 1894): 16, 19.

9. In Kasson, 227.

10. In Alan Trachtenberg, *The Incorporation of America: Culture and Society in the Gilded Age* (New York: Hill & Wang, 2007), 45.

11. Upton Sinclair, *The Jungle* (New York: Doubleday, Page & Co., 1906), 39.

12. Oscar Wilde, "Impressions of America," in *The Prose of Oscar Wilde* (New York: Cosmopolitan Book Corporation, 1919), 699.

13. Fred A. Mackenzie, *The American Invaders: Their Plans, Tactics and Progress* (New York: Street & Smith, 1901), 11–12.

14. In Jackson Lears, *Rebirth of a Nation: The Making of Modern America, 1877–1920.* (New York: HarperCollins, 2009), 201.

15. In Lears, 322.

Selected Bibliography

Note: These are mostly comprehensive secondary sources that tend to cover large parts of the period—and sometimes other periods entirely.

Appleby, Joyce. *The Relentless Revolution: A History of Capitalism.* New York: W.W. Norton, 2010.

Beatty, Jack. *Age of Betrayal: The Triumph of Money in America, 1865–1900.* New York: Alfred A. Knopf, 2007.

Brands, H.W. *American Colossus: The Triumph of Capitalism, 1865–1900.* New York: Doubleday, 2010.

Braverman, Harry. *Labor and Monopoly Capital: The Degradation of Work in the Twentieth Century.* 25th anniversary ed. New York: Monthly Review Press, 1998.

Brown, John K. *The Baldwin Locomotive Works, 1831–1915.* Baltimore: Johns Hopkins University Press, 1995.

Calhoun, Charles W. *From the Bloody Shirt to Full Dinner Pail: The Transformation of Politics and Governance in the Gilded Age.* New York: Hill & Wang, 2010.

Cannato, Vincent J. *American Passage: The History of Ellis Island.* New York: HarperCollins, 2009.

Chandler, Alfred D., Jr. *Scale and Scope: The Dynamics of Industrial Capitalism.* Cambridge, MA: Belknap Press, 1990.

———. *Strategy and Structure: Chapters in the History of American Industrial Enterprise.* Cambridge, MA: MIT Press, 1962.

———. *The Visible Hand: The Managerial Revolution in American Business.* Cambridge, MA: Belknap Press, 1977.

Cronon, Willam. *Nature's Metropolis: Chicago and the Great West.* New York: W.W. Norton, 1991.

Dray, Philip. *There Is Power in a Union.* New York: Doubleday, 2010.

Fox, Stephen. *Transatlantic: Samuel Cunard, Isambard Brunel, and the Great Atlantic Steamships.* New York: HarperCollins, 2003.

Hays, Samuel P. *The Response to Industrialism, 1885–1914.* 2nd ed. Chicago: University of Chicago Press, 1995.

Hofstadter, Richard. *The Age of Reform: From Bryan to F.D.R.* New York: Vintage Books, 1955.

Hounshell, David. *From the American System to Mass Production, 1800–1932.* Baltimore: Johns Hopkins University Press, 1984.

John, Richard R. *Network Nation: Inventing American Telecommunications.* Cambridge, MA: Belknap Press, 2010.

Kasson, John F. *Civilizing the Machine: Technology and Republican Values in America, 1776–1900.* New York: Hill & Wang, 1999.

Kennedy, David M. *Over Here: The First World War and American Society,* 25th anniversary ed. New York: Oxford University Press, 2004.

Lears, Jackson. *No Place of Grace: Antimodernism and the Transformation of American Culture, 1880–1920*. New York: Pantheon Books, 1981.

———. *Rebirth of a Nation: The Making of Modern America, 1877–1920*. New York: HarperCollins, 2009.

Lippmann, Walter. *Drift and Mastery: An Attempt to Diagnose the Current Unrest*. New York: Mitchell Kennerly, 1914.

Misa, Thomas J. *A Nation of Steel*. Baltimore: Johns Hopkins University Press, 1995.

Montgomery, David. *The Fall of the House of Labor: The Workplace, the State and American Labor Activism, 1865–1925*. New York: Cambridge University Press, 1987.

Painter, Nell Irvin. *Standing at Armageddon: The United States, 1877–1919*. New York: W.W. Norton, 1987.

Perry, Claire. *The Great American Hall of Wonders: Art, Science and Invention in the Nineteenth Century*. London: Giles, 2011.

Rhodes, Richard, ed. *Visions of Technology*. New York: Simon & Schuster, 1999.

Richardson, Heather Cox. *West from Appomattox*. New Haven: Yale University Press, 2007.

Schuster, David G. *Neurasthenic Nation: America's Search for Health, Happiness and Comfort, 1869–1920*. New Brunswick: Rutgers University Press, 2011.

Scranton, Philip. *Endless Novelty: Specialty Production and American Industrialization, 1865–1925*. Princeton: Princeton University Press, 1997.

Smith, Page. *The Rise of Industrial America*. New York: McGraw Hill, 1984.

Solnit, Rebecca. *River of Shadows: Eadweard Muybridge and the Technological Wild West*. New York: Penguin, 2004.

Trachtenberg, Alan. *The Incorporation of America: Culture and Society in the Gilded Age*. New York: Hill & Wang, 2007.

Watts, Stephen. *The People's Tycoon: Henry Ford and the American Century*. New York: Random House, 2005.

Weibe, Robert H. *The Search for Order, 1877–1920*. New York: Hill & Wang, 1967.

White, Richard. *Railroaded: The Transcontinentals and the Making of Modern America*. New York: W.W. Norton, 2011.

Index

About the Author

Jonathan Rees is Professor of History at Colorado State University–Pueblo, where he specializes in the history of labor, business, and technology. He is the author of *Representation and Rebellion: The Rockefeller Plan at the Colorado Fuel and Iron Company, 1865–1942*, and of a forthcoming study of the American ice and refrigeration industries. He lives in Pueblo, Colorado, with his wife and two children.